THROUGH THE WINDOW

THROUGH THE WINDOW

Seventeen Essays
(and one short story)

Julian Barnes

VINTAGE BOOKS

London

Published by Vintage 2012

2 4 6 8 10 9 7 5 3 1

First published in Great Britain in 2012 by
Vintage
Random House, 20 Vauxhall Bridge Road,
London SW1V 2SA

www.vintage-books.co.uk

Addresses for companies within The Random House Group
Limited can be found at:
www.randomhouse.co.uk/offices.htm

The Random House Group Limited Reg. No. 954009

A CIP catalogue record for this book
is available from the British Library

ISBN 9780099578581

The Random House Group Limited supports The Forest
Stewardship Council (FSC®), the leading international forest
certification organisation. Our books carrying the FSC label are
printed on FSC® certified paper. FSC is the only forest certification
scheme endorsed by the leading environmental organisations,
including Greenpeace. Our paper procurement policy can
be found at www.randomhouse.co.uk/environment

Typeset in Bembo by Palimpsest Book Production Limited,
Falkirk, Stirlingshire
Printed and bound by CPI Group (UK) Ltd, Croydon CR0 4YY

FOR PAT

CONTENTS

PREFACE

A SEMPÉ CARTOON set in a second-hand bookshop. An upstairs room, shelves of books from floor to ceiling; bare boards, no customers, a lampshade hanging. On the right, the assembled offerings of HISTORY. On the left, mirroring ranks of PHILOSOPHY. Straight ahead there is a similar section, but pierced by a window, through which we can look down onto a street corner. Coming towards it from the left is a little man wearing a hat. Coming towards it from the right is a little woman, also wearing a hat. They cannot see one another, but from our vantage point we can tell they are about to meet, perhaps bump into one another. Something is about to happen, and be witnessed. This section of the bookshop is called FICTION.

This, simply put, in graphic form, is what I have always believed, as a reader and as a novelist. Fiction, more than any other written form, explains and expands life. Biology, of course, also explains life; so do biography and biochemistry and biophysics and biomechanics and biopsychology. But all the biosciences yield to biofiction. Novels tell us the most truth about life: what it is, how we live it, what it might be for, how we enjoy and value it, how it goes wrong, and how we lose it. Novels speak to and from the mind, the heart, the eye, the genitals, the skin; the conscious and the subconscious. What it is to be an individual, what it means to be part of a society. What it means to be alone. Alone, and yet in company: that is the paradoxical position of the reader. Alone in the company of a writer who speaks in the silence of your mind.

And — a further paradox — it makes no difference whether that writer is alive or dead. Fiction makes characters who have never existed as real as your friends, and makes dead writers as alive as a television newsreader.

So most of the pieces in this book are about fiction and its associated forms: the narrative poem, the essay, the translation. How it works and why it works and when it doesn't. We are, in our deepest selves, narrative animals; also, seekers of answers. The best fiction rarely provides answers; but it does formulate the questions exceptionally well.

J.B.
March 2012

THE DECEPTIVENESS OF
PENELOPE FITZGERALD

A FEW YEARS BEFORE her death, I appeared on a panel at York University with Penelope Fitzgerald. I knew her slightly, and admired her greatly. Her manner was shy and rather distrait, as if the last thing she wanted was to be taken for what she then was: the best living English novelist. So she comported herself as if she were some harmless jam-making grandmother who scarcely knew her way in the world. This wasn't too difficult, given that she was indeed a grand-mother, and also – one of the minor revelations in her collected letters – a jam (and chutney) maker. But the disguise wasn't convincing, since every so often, as if despite herself, her rare intelligence and instinctive wit would break through. Over coffee I asked her to sign my two favourite novels of hers: *The Beginning of Spring* and *The Blue Flower*. She hunted around for a long while in the heavy plastic carrier bag – purple, with a floral design, I remember – which contained her day's requirements. A fountain pen was eventually discovered, and after considerable pausing and reflection, she wrote – as it seemed, as I hoped – a private, encouraging message to a younger novelist on each title page. I put the books away without looking at the inscriptions.

The event proceeded. Afterwards, we were driven to York station to travel back to London together. When invited, I had been given the option of a modest fee and standard-class travel, or no fee and a first-class ticket. I had chosen the latter.

The train drew in. I assumed that the university could not possibly have given an octogenarian of such literary distinction anything other than a first-class ticket. But when I set off towards what I assumed to be our carriage, I saw that she was heading in a more modest direction. Naturally, I joined her. I can't remember what we talked about on the journey down; perhaps I mentioned the odd coincidence that we had each made our first hardcover fictional appearance in the same book (*The Times Anthology of Ghost Stories*, 1975); probably I asked the usual daft questions about what she was working on and when the next novel would appear (I later learned that she frequently lied to interviewers). At King's Cross I suggested that we share a cab, since we both lived in the same part of north London. Oh no, she replied, she would take the Underground – after all, she had been given this splendid free travel pass by the Mayor of London (she made it sound like a personal gift, rather than something every pensioner got). Assuming she must be feeling the day even longer than I did, I pressed again for the taxi option, but she was quietly obstinate, and came up with a clinching argument: she had to pick up a pint of milk on the way from the Underground station, and if she went home by cab it would mean having to go out again later. I ploddingly speculated that we could very easily stop the taxi outside the shop and have it wait while she bought her milk. 'I hadn't thought of that,' she said. But no, I still hadn't convinced her: she had decided to take the Underground, and that was that. So I waited beside her on the concourse while she looked for her free pass in the tumult of her carrier bag. It must be there, surely, but no, after much dredging, it didn't seem to be findable. I was by this point feeling – and perhaps exhibiting – a certain impatience, so I marched us to the ticket machine, bought our tickets, and squired her down the escalator to the Northern Line. As we waited for the train, she turned to me with an expression of gentle concern. 'Oh dear,' she said, 'I

do seem to have involved you in some low forms of transport.'
I was still laughing by the time I got home and opened her
books to read those long-pondered inscriptions. In *The
Beginning of Spring* she had written 'best wishes – Penelope
Fitzgerald'; while in *The Blue Flower* – a dedication that had
taken considerably more thought – she had put 'best wishes
– Penelope'.

Like her personal manner, her life and literary career
seemed designed to wrong-foot, to turn attention away from
the fact that she was, or would turn into, a great novelist.
True, she came from a cultured background, having one
father and three uncles among the multi-talented Knox
brothers, whose communal biography she later wrote. Her
father was editor of *Punch*; her mother, one of the first
students at Somerville College, Oxford, also wrote. Penelope
was in turn a brilliant student at Somerville: one of her finals
examiners was so astounded by her papers that he asked his
fellow dons if he could keep them, and later, apparently, had
them bound in vellum. But after this public proof of distinction, throughout what might for others have been their best
writing years, she became a wife and working mother (at
Punch, the BBC, the Ministry of Food, then in journalism
and teaching). She was fifty-eight by the time she published
her first book, a biography of Burne-Jones. She then wrote
a comic thriller, *The Golden Child*, supposedly to amuse her
dying husband. In the period 1975–84 she published two
more biographies and four more novels. Those four novels
are all short, and written close to her own experiences: of
running a bookshop, living on a houseboat, working for the
BBC in wartime, teaching at a stage school. They are adroit,
odd, highly pleasurable, but modest in ambition. And with
almost any other writer you might think that, having used
up her own life, she would – being now in her very late
sixties – have called it a day. On the contrary: over the next
decade, from 1986 to 1995, she published the four novels

– *Innocence*, *The Beginning of Spring*, *The Gate of Angels* and *The Blue Flower* – by which she will be remembered. They are written far from her obvious life, being set, respectively, in 1950s Florence, pre-revolutionary Moscow, Cambridge in 1912 and late-eighteenth-century Prussia. Many writers start by inventing away from their lives, and then, when their material runs out, turn back to more familiar sources. Fitzgerald did the opposite, and by writing away from her own life she liberated herself into greatness.

Even so, when public recognition came, it followed no obvious trajectory, and was attended by a marked level of male diminishment. In 1977 her non-fiction publisher, Richard Garnett, informed her dunderheadedly that she was 'only an amateur writer', to which she replied mildly, 'I asked myself, how many books do you have to write and how many semicolons do you have to discard before you lose amateur status?' The following year, after having been short-listed for the Booker Prize with *The Bookshop*, she asked her fiction publisher, Colin Haycraft, if it would be a good idea to write another novel. He jocundly replied that if she went on writing fiction he didn't want it blamed on him, and in any case already had too many short novels with sad endings on his hands. (Unsurprisingly, Fitzgerald took herself off to another publisher, and Haycraft claimed he had been misunderstood.) I remember Paul Theroux telling me how, as a Booker judge in 1979, he had been doing his preliminary reading while travelling through Patagonia by train, and books he considered not even worth discussing would be skimmed out of the window into the passing pampas. Some months later he found himself with a polite smile on his face as the prize was awarded to Fitzgerald for *Offshore*. The BBC's resident bookheads also treated her condescendingly: radio's Frank Delaney told her she 'deserved to win because my book was free of objectionable matter and suitable for family reading'; while television's Robert Robinson gave her patronisingly little airtime on *The Book Programme* and scarcely concealed his view that she shouldn't have won. And after she died, even her memorial meeting was disfigured by the turkey-cocking of a young male novelist.

You could perhaps argue that she won the Booker with the 'wrong' novel – which would hardly be revolutionary in the history of the prize – though the real dishonour was that she failed to win it again for any of her last four novels. *The Blue Flower*, chosen more times than any other as Book of the Year in 1995, was not even shortlisted – the prize going that year to Pat Barker's *The Ghost Road*. However, Fitzgerald did have a few happy memories of her Booker victory night: 'The best was when the editor of the *Financial Times*, who was on my table, looked at the cheque and said to the Booker McC chairman, "Hmph, I see you've changed your chief cashier." Both their faces were alight with interest.'

There are many such moments in her letters – moments when the professional observer of human beings finds sustenance and reward where others might find boredom or rudeness. Her life, on this evidence, was largely domestic, frequently peripatetic, and attended by regular economic crises. The magazine she edited, *World Review*, collapsed; her husband Desmond had trouble with drink; the houseboat they lived on sank not just once but twice, carrying with it such archives as she possessed (including all her wartime letters to her husband). Rescue at one point came in the shape of a council flat in Clapham, where the novelist collected Green Shield stamps and used tea bags to dye her hair. Her writing had to be fitted into the occasional breathing spaces left by family life; and she made little money until the late success of *The Blue Flower* in America (where it won a National Book Critics Circle Award in the first year the prize was opened to non-nationals). It was a matter of rueful pride to her – and should serve as a warning to aspirant novelists – that she didn't pass into the higher tax bracket until she was

eighty. She was also accident-prone, given to falling off ladders
and out of windows, getting herself locked in the bathroom
and suffering other obscurer incidents ('I was knocked down
by a bus queue and have a round bruise on my arm, just like
the mark of Cain'). She tended to take the blame for things
that were not her fault, even feeling guilty towards her
publishers when her books didn't sell. Nor did she like to
offend: on one occasion, she went to vote, and as she left the
polling station, 'to my disgust the Conservative lady outside
snatched away my card, saying, "I'm only taking *ours*, dear"
– I didn't like to say I was Liberal for fear of hurting her
feelings – she had put a nice green hat on and everything
– I often see her in church.'

That 'nice green hat' is a pure writer's touch; and her
spirit of fantasy is often waiting to transform observed reality.
This is from one of her wartime letters:

> I have had my brother on a week's leave. He slept in
> the passage, and the Danish cook evidently regarded
> him as a soldier billetted on us and ran the carpet-
> sweeper over him remorselessly.

The logical implication being that this would have been quite
normal (if Danish) behaviour had her brother indeed been
such a billetee. There is, at times, something more than a little
Pooterish about the life she describes. Thus: 'I have been
mending my sandals with plastic wood (unfortunately Woolie's
only had "antique walnut") and rather good new plastic soles,
also from Woolie's.' But it is Pooterishness with a difference:
first, it is self-aware; and second, there is a high-boho dash to
it. She knew what she was doing, and writing. At the same
time, this *was* her life.

Alongside the mildness and the blame-taking, however,
there lay a clear moral sense and a sharp dismissal of those
she found wanting. Robert Skidelsky is 'this absurdly irritating

man', Lord David Cecil's lecture on Rossetti was '*abysmal*', Rushdie's latest novel is 'a load of codswallop'. Then there is 'the dread Malcolm Bradbury', who 'seems to be made of some plastic or semi-fluid substance which gives way or changes in your hands', and who patronises her work ('I felt like throwing the pale green mayonnaise over him'); or Douglas Hurd, Booker Prize chairman, with his pitiful notion of what a novel should be. Of Peter Ackroyd's life of Dickens, she merely notes, with mild wryness, 'I don't see how a life of Dickens written by someone who has no sense of humour whatever can be a success.' And here she is on her own critical standing: 'I'm said to be of the school of Beryl Bainbridge which is a good correction to vanity, I expect.'

'On the whole,' she told her American editor in 1987, 'I think you should write biographies of those you admire and respect, and novels about human beings who you think are sadly mistaken.' Fitzgerald is tender towards her characters and their worlds, unpredictably funny, and at times surprisingly aphoristic; though it is characteristic of her that such moments of wisdom appear not author-generated, but arising in the text organically, like moss or coral. Her fictional personnel are rarely vicious or deliberately evil; when things go wrong for them, or when they inflict harm on others, it is usually out of misplaced understanding, a lack less of sympathy than of imagination. The main problem is that they cannot see the terms and conditions which come attached to life: moral grace and social incompetence are often in close proximity. As Salvatore, the neurologist in her 'Italian' novel *Innocence*, puts it, 'There are dilettantes in human relationships just as there are, let's say, in politics.' The aristocratic family into which he is to marry, the Ridolfis, have 'a tendency to rash decisions, perhaps always intended to ensure other people's happiness'. Such people tend to think that love is sufficient in itself, and that happiness might be its merited consequence. They speak their minds at the wrong time and in the wrong way; they deal in a kind of robustly harmful innocence. It is a quality shared equally between the sexes, but not mutually recognised. Thus Salvatore – unaware of his own, more intellectual forms of naivety – is driven to exasperation by the strength and sheer carelessness of the innocence displayed by the two women in his life:

> He struggled to keep his temper. It struck him that both Marta and Chiara took advantage of him by attacking him with their ignorance, or call it innocence. A serious thinking adult had no defence against inno-cence because he was obliged to respect it, whereas the innocent scarcely knows what respect is or ser-iousness either.

Fitzgerald's deep understanding of the complexities and ramifications of innocence makes the children in her fiction not just convincing simulacra, but active motors in the plot. In 1996 an old friend, Hugh Lee, made the bizarre complaint that he found her fictional children 'precious'. Denying this, she replied: 'They're exactly like my own children, who always noticed everything.' And, having noticed, would voice innocence's damaging truths. In 1968 the novelist reported a conversation with – or rather, denunciation by – her younger daughter:

> Maria has much depressed me by 1. Looking at Daddy and me and saying 'What a funny old couple you are!' and 2. Telling me that studying art and literature is only a personal indulgence and doesn't really help humanity or lead to anything, and, I suppose, really, that is quite true: she said it very kindly. My life seems to be crumbling into dust.

It is at such moments that writers have a small advantage over non-writers: the painful moment can at least be stored for later use. Twenty years on, here is Dolly, the plain-speaking young daughter of Frank Reid, owner of a printing works in pre-revolutionary Moscow. When Frank's wife Nellie inexplicably abandons the family and returns to London, Frank asks Dolly if she wants to write to her mother. Dolly replies, 'I don't think I ought to write.' Frank, whose innocence means that he is devoid of self-righteousness, asks, 'Why not, Dolly? Surely you don't think she did the wrong thing?' Dolly gives him a reply neither he nor we expect: 'I don't know whether she did or not. The mistake she probably made was getting married in the first place.'

Many readers' initial reaction to a Fitzgerald novel – especially one of the last four – is, 'But how does she know that?' How does she know (*The Beginning of Spring*) about methods of bribing the police in pre-revolutionary Moscow, and about techniques of printing, and that all packs of playing cards were confiscated at the Russian border? How does she know (*Innocence*) about neurology and dressmaking and dwarfism and Gramsci? How does she know (*The Gate of Angels*) about atomic physics and probationary nursing and the opening of Selfridges? How does she know (*The Blue Flower*) about eighteenth-century Thuringian laundry habits and the Brownian system and Schlegel's philosophy and salt-mining? The initial, dully obvious answer is: she found out. A. S. Byatt once asked her the last of these questions, and received the answer that Fitzgerald 'had read the records of the salt mines from cover to cover in German to understand how her hero was employed'. But when we are asking 'How did she know?' we are really also asking 'But how does she do that?' – how does she convey what she knows in such a compact, exact, dynamic and resonant way? She had a novelist's (and a shy person's) fear of being boringly informative: 'I always feel the reader is very insulted by being told too much,' she said. But it is more than just a taste for economy. It is the art of using fact and detail so that it becomes greater than the sum of its parts. *The Blue Flower* opens with a famous scene of washday in a large house, with all the dirty bedlinen and shirts and undergarments being thrown down from the windows into the courtyard. When remembering this scene and its density of effect, I always think it must last a whole chapter – even though, in a Fitzgerald novel, that need mean no more than seven or eight pages. But whenever I check, I find that in fact it lasts less than two pages – pages which, alongside this domestic scene-setting, also manage to announce key themes of German Romantic philosophy and inconvenient love. I have reread this scene many times, always trying to find its secret, but never succeeding.

Mastery of sources and a taste for concision might lead you to expect that the narrative line of Fitzgerald's novels would be pre-eminently lucid. Far from it: there is a kind of benign wrong-footingness at work, often from the first line. Here is the start of *The Beginning of Spring*:

> In 1913 the journey from Moscow to Charing Cross, changing at Warsaw, cost fourteen pounds, six shillings and threepence and took two and a half days.

This sounds almost journalistically clear, and it is in a way, until you reflect that almost any other novelist would have started a Russian novel featuring mainly English personnel by having a character travel – and so take the reader with him or her – from London to Moscow. Penelope Fitzgerald does the opposite: she opens with a character leaving the very city where all the action is going to take place. But the sentence seems so straightforward that you hardly notice what is being done to you. And here is the first line of *The Blue Flower*:

> Jacob Dietmahler was not such a fool that he could not see that they had arrived at his friend's home on the washday.

Again, another novelist would have been content to write 'Jacob Dietmahler could see that they had arrived . . .' – altogether more banal. A double negative in the first sentence trips our expectation of uncomplicated entry into a novel; further, it sets up the narrative question 'So in that case, just what degree of a fool *was* Jacob Dietmahler?' Also, Fitzgerald writes 'on the washday', where others would be content with the normal English 'on washday'. The definite article hints quietly at the German behind it – *am Waschtag* – and lets us feel, at a nearly subtextual level, that we are in a different time, a different place. It eases our fictional way. For that is one initially puzzling aspect of these last four novels: they do not feel anything like 'historical novels', if historical novels are books in which we as modern readers are transported back in time thanks to a writer instructing us in the necessary background and foreground. Rather, they feel like novels which just happen to be set in history, and which we enter on equal terms with the characters we find within them: it is as if we are reading them in the time they are set, rather than now – and yet we remain in our own period.

Fitzgerald's benign wrong-footingness culminates in scenes where the whole world, as physically experienced and relied upon, is given a sudden tilt. At the start of *The Gate of Angels* a violent rainstorm turns Cambridge upside down – 'tree-tops on the earth, legs in the air, in a university city devoted to logic and reason'; while at that novel's end, the titular gate miraculously opens in what might be a quasi-religious moment, or an outrageous plot device lifted from ghost stories – or, perhaps, both. Then there is that epiphanic scene near the end of *The Beginning of Spring*. Dolly wakes in the middle of the night at the family dacha to find Lisa, the temporary (Russian) governess to the Reid children, dressed to go out; reluctantly, she takes Dolly with her. They walk down a path away from the light in the dacha's front window until a moment when, 'although the path seemed to run quite straight, the light disappeared'. The forest closes in on them. Among the birch stems Dolly begins to see 'what looked like human hands, moving to touch each other across the whiteness and blackness'. In a clearing, men and women stand pressed each against the trunk of a tree. Lisa explains to the tree-people that, although she knows they have come there on her account, she can't stay; she must go back with the child. "'If she speaks about this, she won't be believed. If she remembers it, she'll understand in time what she's seen."' They go back along the path, and Dolly returns to bed; but the forest has invaded the dacha. 'She could still smell the potent leaf-sap of the birch trees. It was as strong inside the house as out.' Does Dolly understand what she's seen – and do we? Is the scene – for which we have only the child's point of view – a dream, a hallucination, the memory of a sleepwalker? If not, what is its register? Are the woods coming to life, as they do in the pantheistic poetry of Selwyn Crane, the novel's Tolstoyan dreamer? Does the scene symbolise female awakening or personal liberation, for Dolly, or for Lisa, or both? Perhaps Dolly has witnessed the preparations for some pagan rite of spring (only a few pages later, Stravinsky's name is quietly mentioned). Or might the secret meeting in the forest be straightforwardly political, even revolutionary (Lisa, we later discover, is a politico)? Some, even all these interpretations are possible, and, mysteriously, not incompatible with one another. This short passage occupies a mere three pages of text, but, as with the laundry scene in *The Blue Flower*, it expands into something much larger in the memory. And again we ask ourselves: how does she do that?

One of our better-known novelists once described the experience of reading a Fitzgerald novel as riding along in a top-quality car, only to find that after a mile or so, 'someone throws the steering-wheel out of the window'; another, while praising *The Beginning of Spring*, called it 'scatty'. These judgements seem to me profoundly misconceived. In *The Beginning of Spring*, there is a scene in which Frank Reid reflects briefly on the Russian system of bribery. There has been a break-in at his press; the malefactor fires a revolver at Reid, who apprehends him, but decides not to report the matter to the police. However, he fails to offer the street's nightwatchman, who must have been aware of the incident, a hundred roubles, 'somewhere between tea-money and a bribe', for his silence. As a result, the watchman goes to the police:

> From them he would have got considerably less, but very likely he needed the money immediately. Probably he was caught in the tight network of small loans, debts, repayments and foreclosures which linked the city, quarter by quarter, in its grip, as securely as the tram-lines themselves.

Novels are like cities: some are organised and laid out with the colour-coded clarity of public transport maps, with each chapter marking a progress from one station to the next, until all the characters have been successfully carried to their thematic terminus. Others, the subtler, wiser ones, offer no such immediately readable route maps. Instead of a journey through the city, they throw you into the city itself, and life itself: you are expected to find your own way. And their structure and purpose may not be immediately apparent, being based on the tacit network of 'loans, debts, repayments and foreclosures' that makes up human relationships. Nor do such novels move mechanically; they stray, they pause, they lollop, as life does, except with a greater purpose and hidden structure. A priest in *The Beginning of Spring*, seeking to assert the legibility of God's purpose in the world, says, 'There are no accidental meetings.' The same is true of the best fiction. Such novels are not difficult to read, since they are so filled with detail and incident and the movement of life, but they are sometimes difficult to work out. This is because the absentee author has the confidence to presume that the reader might be as subtle and intelligent as she is. Penelope Fitzgerald's novels are pre-eminent examples of this kind.

THE 'UNPOETICAL' CLOUGH

IN APRIL 1849, a thirty-year-old English poet arrived in Rome. British writers had been coming here on a regular basis for a century and more. In 1764, the city's effect on Gibbon was so powerful that 'several days of intoxication were lost or enjoyed before I could descend to a cool and minute investigation'. In 1818 Shelley found its monuments 'sublime'. The following year the city 'delighted' Byron: 'it beats Greece – Constantinople – everything – at least that I have ever seen'. And in 1845 Dickens arrived for his first visit, later telling his biographer John Forster that he had been 'moved and over-come' by the Colosseum as by no other sight in his life, 'except perhaps by the first contemplation of the Falls of Niagara'.

The young English poet was in good spirits, and happier than at any previous time in his adult life. His great early crisis – one mixing religious belief and employment, and causing him to resign his fellowship at Oxford because he could no longer subscribe to the XXXIX Articles – was over; a post at University College, London awaited him in the autumn. He was a classicist as well as a poet, and so we might expect Rome to produce a similar effect on him as it had on his literary predecessors. But neither the city of the ancient Romans nor that of the modern popes impressed him. He wrote to his mother:

> St Peter's disappoints me: the stone of which it is made is a poor plastery material; and, indeed, Rome in general might be called a *rubbishy* place; the Roman

antiquities in general seem to me only interesting as antiquities, and not for any beauty . . . The weather has not been very brilliant.

If you want a one-word introduction to the tone, sensibility and modernity of Arthur Hugh Clough, you have it in that single, italicised (by him, not me) word: *rubbishy*. He will not subscribe to the required tenets of his country's established religion if his conscience and intellect tell him otherwise; similarly, he will not subscribe to presumptions of grandeur and beauty if his eyes and aesthetic antennae tell him otherwise. Nor was this some initial irreverence, the grumpy consequence of baggage loss or digestive calamity. It was an opinion Clough confirmed by writing it into the opening canto of a poem he composed during his three-month stay in the city:

> *Rome disappoints me much; I hardly as yet understand, but*
> Rubbishy *seems the word that most exactly would*
> *suit it.*
> *All the foolish destructions, and all the sillier savings,*
> *All the incongruous things of past incompatible ages,*
> *Seem to be treasured up here to make fools of present*
> *and future.*
> *Would to Heaven the old Goths had made a cleaner*
> *sweep of it!*
> *Would to Heaven the new ones would come and destroy*
> *these churches!*

Shelley had taken a regular evening walk to the Forum, where he admired the 'sublime desolation of the scene'. Claude, the protagonist of *Amours de Voyage*, remains unmoved:

> *What do I find in the Forum? An archway and two or*
> *three pillars.*

And what of the Colosseum, for Dickens that Niagara-equalling wonder?

> *No one can cavil, I grant, at the size of the*
> *great Coliseum.*
> *Doubtless the notion of grand and capacious and*
> *massive amusement,*
> *This the old Romans had; but tell me, is this an idea?*

Where others find splendour, Claude sees mere solidity:

> *'Brickwork I found thee, and marble I left thee!' their*
> *Emperor vaunted;*
> *'Marble I thought thee, and brickwork I find thee!' the*
> *Tourist may answer.*

Claude, like Clough, is a very un–Grand Tourist. He also finds himself in a city where, after a long slumber, history is beginning to happen again. Two months previously, in February 1849, Mazzini had declared the Roman Republic, which Garibaldi was now preparing to defend. On 22 April, Clough had an audience with Mazzini, handing over to the republic's anglophile triumvir a cigar case, the gift of Carlyle. The next day he wrote to his friend F. T. Palgrave (the future editor of *The Golden Treasury*), describing a visit to the Colosseum. He reported not ageless magnificence, nor even shabby decrepitude, but a thoroughly modern event, a political rally with

> a band somewhere over the entrance playing national hymns. At the end of the great hymn, of which I don't know the name, while the people were clapping, viva-ing and encoring, light began to spread, and all at once the whole amphitheatre was lit up with – the trois couleurs! The basement red fire, the two next stories green, and the plain white of the common

light at the top. Very queer, you will say; but it was
really very fine, and I should think the Colosseum
never looked better . . .

Clough has often been treated as a marginal figure, both
on the university English syllabus and in the English canon.
Most people probably first come across him as the figure of
'Thyrsis' in Matthew Arnold's memorial poem of that name
– which, for a memorial poem, doesn't seem to concentrate
enough on the dead friend (Ian Hamilton called it 'funda-
mentally a condescending, not to say complacent piece of
work'). They might assume he was an Arnoldian poet who
had died prematurely; or, given his authorship of the rousing
'Say Not the Struggle Naught Availeth', put him down for a
typical lesser Victorian. Nothing could be less true, though
changing people's assumptions at this late date isn't easy. I
once spent about five years trying to get a distinguished
professor of English actually to *read* Clough: I sent him the
books, and discovered that his own son was waging a parallel
campaign on the poet's behalf. Even so, this leading scholar
didn't eventually start on Clough until he had retired from
teaching English literature.

The association with Matthew Arnold is misleading. They
were friends and crypto-brothers (the schoolboy Clough, his
family away in America, was taken into the Arnold household);
they followed the same trajectory at Rugby and Oxford; but
it was their differences that marked them. As undergraduates
they even employed different symbols to mark the days when
they succumbed to the 'wretched habit' of masturbation:
Clough used an asterisk in his diary, Arnold a cross. Arnold,
though four years younger, always behaved in letters as if he
were both older and wiser. He judged Clough too excitable,
too politically involved – teasing him as 'Citizen Clough' –
and not standing back, as he himself did, to examine the
'tendency' of nations. When Europe blew up in continent-wide

revolution in 1848, Clough set off for France to witness events at first hand. Arnold would not be 'sucked even for an hour into the Time Stream'. At the height of that year's thrilling events, Arnold sent Clough a copy of the *Bhagavad Gita*, praising its 'reflectiveness and caution'.

Such divergences transfer into their poetry. Arnold comes out of Keatsian Romanticism, Clough out of Byronism – specifically, the sceptical, worldly, witty tone-mixing of *Don Juan*. Nowadays, if you were to set Arnold and Clough anonymously side by side, you might guess there to be a generation or more separating them. Arnold is a sonorous, high-minded poet, one who defends culture against both anarchy and Philistia; but essentially one who refers us backwards, to the canon, to the great tradition of Western civilisation which began in Greece and Rome. Clough was equally aware of that heritage: and when Arnold offered him a prose tribute in his lecture 'On Translating Homer', it was to a poet 'with some admirable Homeric qualities' and a man marked by 'the Homeric simplicity of his literary life'. Yet Arnold is here affiliating, assimilating – and taming – Clough. As he detected a neuroticism in Clough's make-up, a 'loose screw in his whole organisation', so he thought there was also too much instability, too little hard-chiselled beauty, in Clough's poetry. Arnold judged himself simply more poetic and more artistic than Clough, just as Keats had judged himself superior to Byron, whose *Don Juan* he found 'flash'. ('You speak of Lord Byron and me,' he wrote to George Keats. 'There is this great difference between us. He describes what he sees – I describe what I imagine. Mine is the hardest task. You see the immense difference.') Yet what Arnold perceived to be the weaknesses of Clough's poetry are precisely what over time have come to seem its strengths – a prosy colloquiality which at times verges on awkwardness, a preference for honesty and sarcasm over suavity and tact, a direct criticism of modern life, a naming of things as themselves. If Arnold had died before Clough, and Clough had written an elegy for him, the dead friend would more probably have been called 'Matt' than christened after some Virgilian shepherd.

The poem of Arnold's which speaks to us most directly today is 'Dover Beach' (though it was not one he especially rated himself). His analysis of our metaphysical plight in a godless world begins with nature description, proceeds by reference to Sophocles, then declares its central tidal metaphor before coming to its bleak conclusion with a Thucydidean allusion; while the diction by which it leads us there includes phrases such as 'the moon-blanch'd land', 'the folds of a bright girdle furl'd' and (famously) 'a darkling plain'. It is stately, mournful and magnificent. At the same time, compare 'darkling' with 'rubbishy'. Also, compare 'The Latest Decalogue', Clough's own poem about religious belief and what has happened to it. This is cast as a sardonic parody of the Ten Commandments, and its freethinking (or blasphemy) precedes *Life of Brian* by over a century:

> *Thou shalt have one God only; who*
> *Would be at the expense of two?*
> *No graven images may be*
> *Worshipped, except the currency . . .*

It is a poem which undermines both Church and State, and suspects the motives of every churchgoing Christian:

> *Thou shalt not kill; but need'st not strive*
> *Officiously to keep alive:*
> *Do not adultery commit;*
> *Advantage rarely comes of it.*

Mrs Thatcher famously urged us to rediscover 'Victorian values'; Clough had already anatomised those values at the time:

> *Thou shalt not steal; an empty feat,*
> *When it's so lucrative to cheat . . .*
> *Thou shalt not covet; but tradition*
> *Approves all forms of competition.*

Victorian money-culture and money-worship, so success-fully reintroduced into this country over the last thirty years, received further treatment from Clough in *Dipsychus*, the last of his three great long poems. Today's City traders, driving up motorways in flame-red Ferraris, and driving up their bills in Gordon Ramsay restaurants with four-figure wines, have their precise Victorian counterparts:

> *I drive through the street, and I care not a d—mn;*
> *The people they stare, and they ask who I am;*
> *And if I should chance to run over a cad,*
> *I can pay for the damage if ever so bad.*
> > *So pleasant it is to have money, heigh ho!*
> > *So pleasant it is to have money . . .*

> *The best of the tables and best of the fare –*
> *And as for the others, the devil may care;*
> *It isn't our fault if they dare not afford*
> *To sup like a prince and be drunk as a lord.*
> > *So pleasant it is to have money, heigh ho!*
> > *So pleasant it is to have money.*

Amours de Voyage is preceded by four epigraphs. The first three invoke the poem's main themes – self-love, love, doubt, travel – while the fourth, from Horace, announces its manner: 'Flevit amores / Non elaboratum ad pedem' – 'He lamented his loves / In unpolished metre' (though Horace actually wrote 'amorem'). Clough's metre is 'unpolished' compared to Arnold's; and in *Amours de Voyage* – as in his first long poem, *The Bothie of Tober-na-Vuolich* – he uses the rare hexameter.

This has more of a thumping stress than the polished and popular pentameter; but it also helps provide the spontaneous, conversational, unposh tone. Clough's rhythms are travelling, chuntering, stopping-and-starting; he needs to be able to switch direction and tone, move from cultural history to love-gossip in a line, from high analysis to a quick joke. When Clough was planning his first book of poems, Arnold had complained about 'a deficiency of the beautiful', and wrote to Clough: 'I doubt your being an *artist*.' When he published *The Bothie*, Arnold found it too flippant: 'If I were to say the real truth as to your poems in general, as they impress me – it would be this – that they are not *natural*.' (This from Matthew Arnold . . .) He asked Clough to consider 'whether you attain the beautiful' and reminds him on 'how deeply *unpoetical* the age and all one's surroundings are. Not unprofound, not ungrand, not unmoving: but unpoetical.' Arnold's solution was to transcend or transmute – or avoid – the unpoeticality, Clough's to represent it: he is the 'unpoetical' poet.

So *Amours de Voyage* is full of un-Arnoldian personnel – Mazzini, Garibaldi, General Oudinot – and paraphernalia: a copy of Murray's guide and a cry to the waiter for a caffè-latte. It is absolutely contemporary, written at and about a moment when Italy was in the process of being painfully constructed; it includes gunfire and war and one of the finest literary representations of the confusion of murder – the mid-piazza ambush of a priest caught trying to flee the city and join the besieging army:

> You didn't see the dead man? No; – I began to
> be doubtful;
> I was in black myself, and didn't know what
> mightn't happen; –
> But a National Guard close by me, outside of the hubbub,
> Broke his sword with slashing a broad hat covered in
> dust, – and

> *Passing away from the place with Murray under my*
> > > > > > > > *arm, and*
> *Stooping, I saw through the legs of the people the legs of*
> > > > > > > > > > *a body.*

It is also a highly contemplative and argumentative poem, about history, civilisation and the individual's duty to act. And it is, as the title tells us, a love story – or, this being Clough, a sort of modern, near-miss, almost-but-not-quite love story, with mismatching, misunderstanding, tortuous self-searching, and a mad, hopeful, hopeless pursuit leading us to a kind of ending.

Whether any part of Claude's emotional trajectory also happened to Clough – in Rome and places north in that spring and summer of 1849 – is now, happily, unknowable. In any case, Clough sets up his narrator in ways which signal the differences between the two of them. First, Claude is made, in the opening canto, extremely dislikeable: snobbish, superior, world-weary, and deeply patronising to the bourgeois English family (including three unmarried daughters) whom he falls in with. For Claude, the middle classes are 'neither man's aristocracy . . . nor God's'; his snooty nostrils sniff 'the taint of the shop', and he openly admits 'the horrible pleasure of pleasing inferior people'. He is created this way, we assume, so that he may – like Austen's arrogant males – be subsequently tamed and humanised by love of the supposedly inferior. Secondly, Claude is un-Cloughlike both in matters of religion – Claude is suspected of Romanism, while Clough leaned towards unbelief – and of politics. Claude has hitherto avoided public matters and scorned What People Think, preferring a detached, critical, aesthetic attitude to life – in which he is closer to the *Bhagavad Gita*-reading Arnold than to the liberal, event-chasing Clough who now, from Rome, signs another letter to Palgrave '*Le Citoyen malgré lui*'.

The poem's narrative is activated when Claude's

complacent presumptions and foppish idlenesses are suddenly overthrown. The Romans' defence of their new republic against the French Army, who are besieging the city 'to reinstate Pope and Tourist', jolts Claude into the modern world of politics and war; similarly, his exposure to the Trevellyn family, who display all the enthusiasm he lacks ('Rome is a wonderful place', gushes Georgina) jolts him into a state of love, or – he being a self-conscious intellectual – near-love, or possible-love, or a state of mind in which whatever it is that love might be is subjected to furious internal debate. In one reply to his friend Eustace (whose own letters are not given, leaving only Claude's reactions to them – a tactic which jump-cuts the narrative), he corrects a false inference: 'I am in love, you say: I do not think so, exactly.'

At the poem's centre is a debate about 'exact thinking', and how such thinking translates into action, and whether emotion as opposed to reason is ever a justifiable ground for action, and whether action is ever worth it in the first place – though of course if it were to be so, then it must first be based on absolutely exact thinking – and, as any sensible reader will swiftly deduce, this is exactly the sort of overanalytical 'pother' (Claude's word) which is most discouraging to a woman who might be inclined to think that you might be inclined to be in love with her. If Clough's view of Rome is post-Romantic, Claude as a lover relates less to any Byronic predecessors than to those indecisive, self-conscious, paralysed creatures who inhabit nineteenth-century Russian fiction. Claude is 'too shilly-shally', observes Georgina, while he himself comes to regret (in another un-Arnoldian phrase) his 'fiddle-faddling'. Claude epitomises how disastrous it is for a lover to see the other side of the question, and to remind himself of the advantages of not being in love: 'Yet, at the worst of the worst, books and a chamber remain' – a line which is an eerie pre-echo of Larkin's renunciatory 'Poetry of Departures': 'Books; china; a life / Reprehensibly perfect.'

So *Amours de Voyage* – this great long poem which is also a great short novella – is in the end about failure, about not seizing the day, about misreading and overanalysing, about cowardice. But cowardice is generally more interesting to the writer than courage, as failure is more exciting than success; and perhaps – as Claude observes in one of his more chilling rationalisations – perhaps the need for kindness precludes the getting of it.

As for success: *Amours de Voyage* was first published in *The Atlantic Monthly* in 1858; and writers today, as they fret about royalties and advances and reading fees and PLR and copyright and agents and status, might reflect that this was the only occasion in his entire life when Clough received the slightest payment for any poem that he wrote.

GEORGE ORWELL
AND THE FUCKING ELEPHANT

YOU HAVE TO feel a little sorry for Mr and Mrs Vaughan Wilkes, or 'Sambo' and 'Flip' as they were known to their charges. During the first decades of the twentieth century, they ran a preparatory school on the south coast of England. It was no worse than many other such establishments: the food was bad, the building underheated, physical punishment the norm. Pupils learned 'as fast as fear could teach us', as one alumnus later wrote. The day began with a frigid and fetid plunge bath; boys denounced one another to the authorities for homosexual practices; and daily morale was dependent on whether a boy was in or out of favour with Flip. In some ways the school was better than many: it had a good academic record; Sambo nurtured contacts at the most important public schools, especially Eton; and clever boys from decent families were accepted on half fees. This was a calculated act of generosity: in return, the boys were meant to reward the school by gaining academic distinction.

Often, this worked, and the Wilkeses might have had reason to congratulate themselves, in the early years of the First World War, for having admitted on reduced terms the sons of Major Matthew Connolly, a retired army officer, and Richard Blair, a former civil servant in the Opium Department of the government of India. The two boys, Cyril and Eric, each won the Harrow Prize (a nationwide history competition), and then took scholarships to Eton in successive years. The Wilkeses must have thought their investments had paid off, the accounts balanced and closed.

But Englishmen of a certain class – especially those sent away to boarding schools – tend towards obsessive memory, looking back on those immured years either as an expulsion from the familial Eden, and a traumatic introduction to the concept of alien power, or else the opposite, a golden and protected time before life's realities intrude. And so, just as the Second World War was about to begin, the Wilkeses, much to their distaste, became a matter of public discussion and argument. Major Connolly's boy, young Cyril – renamed 'Tim' at St Cyprian's, and given the school character of an Irish rebel (if a tame one) – published *Enemies of Promise*. While describing in some detail the harshness and cruelty of the lightly disguised 'St Wulfric's', Connolly also admitted that, as preparatory schools went, it had been 'a well-run and vigorous example which did me good'. Flip was 'able, ambitious, temperamental and energetic'. Connolly, who leaned towards Edenic moralising (especially about Eton), recalled the vivid pleasures of reading, natural history and homoerotic friendship. He devoted several wistful pages to the latter subject. *Enemies of Promise*, published in 1938, must have felt to the Wilkeses as damaging as the fire which burnt St Cyprian's to the ground the following year. Flip wrote Connolly a 'Dear Tim' letter about the harm he had done to 'two people who did a very great deal for you', adding that the book had 'hurt my husband a lot when he was ill and easily upset'.

For the next thirty years, the debate continued as to the true nature of the Wilkeses – diligent pedagogues or manipulative sadists – and as to the wider consequences of sending small boys away from home at the age of eight: character-building or character-deforming? The photographer Cecil Beaton had been at St Cyprian's at the same time as Connolly and Blair, surviving on charm and the ability to placate by singing 'If you were the only girl in the world, and I were the only boy'. He applauded Connolly for having 'seen through all the futilities and snobbishness of Flip and her entourage'. Others joined in, like the naturalist Gavin Maxwell, and the golf correspondent Henry Longhurst, a stout defender of Flip as 'the most formidable, distinguished and unforgettable woman I am likely to meet in my lifetime'. Connolly later came to regret what he had written. When Flip died in August 1967 at the age of ninety-one, he turned up at her funeral, doubtless expecting sentimental reunion, the rheumy eye and the forgiving handshake. Not a bit of it. The Major's boy had turned out a bad egg and a bounder, as literary types often do. Connolly self-pityingly noted that 'nobody spoke to me'.

Yet Flip's death merely led to the most savage and contentious contribution to the debate. Ten years after *Enemies of Promise*, Eric Blair, by then George Orwell, wrote his essay 'Such, Such Were the Joys', as a pendant to Connolly's account. It was never published in Britain during his lifetime, or Flip's, for fear of libel; but it did come out in the States, in the *Partisan Review*, in 1952. Longhurst picked up a copy of the magazine in Honolulu, and was 'so shocked that I have never read it again'. Forty years after it was first published in Britain, sixty years after it was composed, and now almost a century after the events it describes, 'Such, Such' retains immense force, its clarity of exposition matched by its animating rage. Orwell does not try to backdate his understanding; he retains the inchoate emotional responses of the young Eric Blair to the system into which he had been flung. But now, as George Orwell, he is in a position to anatomise the economic and class infrastructure of St Cyprian's, and those hierarchies of power which the pupil would later meet in grown-up, public, political form: in this respect such schools were truly named 'preparatory'.

Orwell also writes with the unhealed pain of an abused child, a pain which occasionally leaks into the prose. He describes a younger pupil – aristocratic and thus entitled to privileges denied to half-fees Blair – like this: 'a wretched, drivelling little creature, almost an albino, peering upwards out of weak eyes, with a long nose at the end of which a dewdrop always seemed to be trembling'. When this boy had a choking fit at dinner, 'a stream of snot ran out of his nose onto his plate in a horrible way to see. Any lesser person would have been called a dirty little beast and ordered out of the room instantly.' Orwell's denunciatory fervour is counterproductive; readers may well feel sorry for the little chap whose hair colour, nasal explosions and accident of birth were none of his doing.

If Connolly was by his own admission a tame rebel at St Cyprian's, Orwell was a true one: Connolly wrote that Blair 'alone among the boys was an intellectual, and not a parrot'. And if the child is father to the man, the writer's account of his own childhood is often a sure guide to his adult mentality. (At St Cyprian's Blair denounced boys for homosexuality – 'one of the contexts in which it was proper to sneak'. Decades later, during the Cold War, Orwell sneaked on the politically unreliable to the Foreign Office.) 'Such, Such Were the Joys' is about life in an English preparatory school; but it is also about politics, class, Empire and adult psychology. And the writer's mature views on these subjects feed into his corrective vehemence:

> Life was hierarchical and whatever happened was right. There were the strong, who deserved to win and always did win, and there were the weak, who deserved to lose and always did lose, everlastingly.

The same typist who produced the final, fair copy of 'Such, Such' also typed a draft of *Nineteen Eighty-Four*; both the cadences, and the message, of those two sentences must have made her feel the overlap.

The Queen of England, advised by her government, appoints knights and peers; the nation at large, by more informal means, appoints national treasures. To achieve this status, it is not sufficient just to be outstanding in your profession; you need to reflect back some aspect of how the country imagines itself to be. (You also mustn't be seen to be chasing the title too hard.) Typically, national treasures tend to be actors or sportsfolk or, increasingly, those made famous by television. It is hard for living writers to become NTs, but not impossible. Charm is important; so is the capacity not to threaten, not to be obviously clever; you should be perceptive but not too intellectual. A most successful national treasure of the last century was John Betjeman, whose genial, bumbly appearances on television overcame the handicap of his being a poet. Someone like Betjeman's contemporary Evelyn Waugh could never have become a treasure – too rude, too openly contemptuous of those whose opinions he despised. Postulants for treasuredom are allowed to have political views, but must never appear angry, or self-righteous, or superior. In recent times, the two writers to attain unarguable NT status have been John Mortimer and Alan Bennett: both old-fashioned liberals, but managing to exude the sense that if confronted by a rabid crypto-fascist Little Englander, they would offer a glass of champagne (in Mortimer's case) or a steaming mug of cocoa (in Bennett's) and then search for common ground in uncontentious topics.

When it comes to the dead, it is hard to retain, or posthumously acquire, treasuredom. Being a Great Writer in itself has little to do with the matter. The important factors are: 1) An ambassadorial quality, an ability to present the nation to itself, and represent it abroad, in a way it wishes to be presented and represented. 2) An element of malleability and interpretability. The malleability allows the writer to be given a more appealing, if not entirely untruthful, image; the interpretability means that we can all find in him or her more or less whatever we require. 3) The writer, even if critical of his or her country, must have a patriotic core, or what appears to be one.

Thus Dickens, as Orwell observed, is 'one of those writers who are worth stealing' (by 'Marxists, by Catholics and, above all, by Conservatives'). He also fulfils criterion 3: 'Dickens attacked English institutions with a ferocity that has never since been approached. Yet he managed to do it without making himself hated, and, more than this, the very people he attacked have swallowed him so completely that he has become a national institution himself.' Something similar has happened with Trollope, who – partly through relentless TV adaptations, but also because he invented the pillar box – hovers on the edge of being a national treasure. This near-status has been greatly helped by the public support of two Trollope-reading Tory prime ministers, Harold Macmillan and John Major – despite the fact that Trollope hated Tories.

And George Orwell? It would surprise, and doubtless irritate, him to discover that since his death in 1950 he has moved implacably towards NT status. He is interpretable, malleable, ambassadorial and patriotic. He denounced the Empire, which pleases the left; he denounced communism, which pleases the right. He warned us against the corrupting effect on politics and public life of the misuse of language, which pleases almost everyone. He said that 'Good prose is like a windowpane', which pleases those who, despite living in the land of Shakespeare and Dickens, mistrust 'fancy' writing.* He was dubious of anyone who was too 'clever'. (This is a key English suspicion, most famously voiced in 1961 when Lord Salisbury, a stalwart of the imperialist Tory right, denounced Iain Macleod, Secretary of State for the Colonies

---

*Airport novelists irritated by their lack of status (a spectacle as comic as literary novelists moaning about their sales) habitually invoke one of two comparisons to prove their own worth: Dickens, who would have applauded their broad appeal, and Orwell, who would have approved their 'plain' (i.e. banal) style.

and member of the new reforming Tory left, as 'too clever by half'.) Orwell used 'sophisticated' and 'intellectual' and 'intelligentsia' as terms of dispraise, hated Bloomsbury, and not just expected but hoped that the sales of *Uncle Tom's Cabin* would outlast those of Virginia Woolf. He was scathing about social elites, finding the ruling class 'stupid'. In 1941 he declared that Britain was the most class-ridden country on earth, ruled by 'the old and silly', 'a family with the wrong members in control'; yet he also recognised that the ruling class was '*morally* fair and sound' and in time of war 'ready enough to get themselves killed'. He describes the condition of the working class with sympathy and rage, thought them wiser than intellectuals, but didn't sentimentalise them; in their struggle they were as 'blind and stupid' as a plant struggling towards the light.

Orwell is profoundly English in even more ways than these. He is deeply untheoretical and wary of general conclusions that do not come from specific experiences. He is a moralist and puritan, one who, for all his populism and working-class sympathies, is squeamish about dirt, disgusted by corporeal and faecal odours. He is caricatural of Jews to the point of anti-Semitism, and routinely homophobic, using 'the pansy left' and 'nancy poets' as if they were accepted sociological terms. He dislikes foreign food, and thinks the French know nothing about cooking; while the sight of a gazelle in Morocco makes him dream of mint sauce. He lays down stern rules about how to make and drink tea, and in a rare sentimental flight imagines the perfect pub. He is uninterested in creature comforts, clothes, fashion, sport, frivolity of any kind, unless that frivolity – like seaside postcards or boys' magazines – leads to some broader social rumination. He likes trees and roses, and barely mentions sex. His preferred literary form, the essay, is quintessentially English. He is a one-man, truth-telling awkward squad, and what, the English like to pretend, could be more English than that? Finally, when he rebranded himself, he took the Christian name of England's patron saint. There aren't too many Erics in the lists either of saints or of national treasures. The only St Eric is Swedish, and he wasn't even a proper, Pope-made saint.

'Getting its history wrong', wrote Ernest Renan, 'is part of being a nation.' Pointedly, he said 'being' not 'becoming': the self-delusion is a constant requirement, not just part of a state's initial creation myth. Similarly, getting its iconic figures wrong – and rebranding them at intervals – is part of being a nation. The Orwell whom the English have sanctified is a descendant of the stone-kicking, beef-eating, commonsensical Dr Johnson (another malleable iconic construct). It is the Orwell who writes to the publisher Frederic Warburg in October 1948, 'I think Sartre is a bag of wind and I am going to give him a big boot.' It is the Orwell of straight thinking, plain writing, moral clarity and truth-telling. Yet things are never quite so simple, not even in the truth-telling, and Orwell's own line – 'All art is to some extent propaganda' – should make us cautious (and reflect that the dictum applies a fortiori to journalism). Take Orwell's denunciation of St Cyprian's. Despite being written three decades after young Eric Blair's grim experiences, it is much harsher than that of anyone else who wrote about the school. If Orwell had lived to show up at Flip's funeral, the revenge of the golf correspondents might have been worthy of St Cyprian's itself. But was Orwell's account so unremitting because he saw more truth than all the others, because time had not sentimentalised him, because with hindsight he could see exactly how that kind of education system perverted young minds and spirits to the wider purposes of the British Establishment and Empire? And/or was his thumb propagandistically on the scale?

One small moment of literary history at which many Orwellians would like to have been present was an encounter in Bertorelli's restaurant between Orwell's biographer, Bernard Crick, and Orwell's widow, Sonia. Crick dared to doubt the utter truthfulness of one of Orwell's most celebrated pieces of reportage, 'Shooting an Elephant'. Sonia, 'to the delight of other clients', according to Crick, 'screamed' at him across the table, 'Of course he shot a fucking elephant. He said he did. Why do you always doubt his fucking word!' The widow, you feel, was screaming for England. Because what England wants to believe about Orwell is that, having seen through the dogma and false words of political ideologies, he refuted the notion that facts are relative, flexible, or purpose-serving; further, he taught us that even if 100 per cent truth is unobtainable, then 67 per cent is and always will be better than 66 per cent, and that such a small percentage point is a morally non-negotiable unit.

But the unpatriotic doubter must persist, and Crick did. And in the afterword to the paperback edition of his biography he quotes a tape recording of an old Burma hand's memories of the incident Orwell recounted. According to the elderly witness, Orwell did indeed shoot 'a fucking elephant'. However, the elephant had not, as Orwell claimed, rampagingly killed a man (whose corpse he described in detail); further, since the beast had been valuable company property, not to be so lightly destroyed, its owners complained to the government, whereupon Blair was packed off to a distant province, and a certain Colonel Welbourne called him 'a disgrace to Eton College'. Such external doubting might corroborate the internal doubts of literary genre. As Crick argues, twelve of the fourteen pieces in the issue of *Penguin New Writing* where 'Shooting an Elephant' first appeared were 'similarly of a then fashionable genre that blurred the line between fact and fiction – the documentary "authentic style"'.

The same scepticism – or critical research – may be, and has been, applied to Orwell's equally celebrated anti-Empire piece, 'A Hanging'. Crick, while admiring its six pages as having 'the terror of Goya coupled with the precise, mundane observation of Sickert', was not convinced that Orwell had ever attended a hanging; or even if he had, whether it was *this* one – the hanging of the essay being by implication something confected. Whether or not this is the case, there is one interesting omission from Orwell's account: any stated reason why the man was being hanged. If, as a young journalist, you attended an execution, and afterwards drank whisky with those in charge, you would surely have found out what crime the poor devil had supposedly committed. And if so, why not pass it on to your readers? It's possible that the offence was so vile that Orwell suppressed it lest readers conclude that there might, after all, be something to be said for capital punishment. Or he might have suppressed it as irrelevant, given his belief that any execution anywhere was 'an unspeakable wrongness'. Or, as Crick suspected, he might have been describing a typical execution rather than a specific one.

When Dirk Bogarde or Ronald Reagan exaggerate (or invent) their war service, we think them mildly (or seriously) deluded. We might, if sympathetic, imagine them stretching the truth once or twice, and then finding themselves stuck with the story they had concocted. Why judge Orwell differently? Because he's Orwell. We could argue, as David Lodge has done with 'A Hanging', that the value of the two Burmese pieces does not rest on their being factually true. But this is a very literary defence, and possibly a case of cutting the writer more slack because we admire him anyway. Yet we are hardly dealing with someone like Ford Madox Ford, who believed in the greater truth of impressions over that of mere grubby facts; and if the neglected Ford is sometimes classified as a 'writer's writer', the sanctified Orwell was the very opposite – a kind of non-writer's writer. Sometimes the naive reaction is the correct one. Many of those who admire him might lose respect or faith if he turned out not to have shot a fucking elephant, or not to have attended this specific fucking execution, because he, George Orwell, said he had, and if he hadn't, then was he not mirroring those political truth-twisters whom he denounced? If 'all art is to some extent propaganda', then are we not to suppose that the laws of propaganda apply even if you are on the side of truth, justice and the angels?

One of the effects of reading Orwell's essays en masse is to realise how very dogmatic – in the non-ideological sense – he is. This is another aspect of his Johnsonian Englishness. From the quotidian matter of how to make a cup of tea to the socio-economic analysis of the restaurant (an entirely unnecessary luxury, to Orwell's puritanical mind), he is a law-giver, and his laws are often founded in disapproval. He is a great writer *against*. So his 'Bookshop Memories' – a subject others might turn into a gentle colour piece with a few amusing anecdotes – scorns lightness. The work, he declares, is drudgery, quite unrewarding, and makes you hate books; while the customers tend to be thieves, paranoiacs, dimwits or, at best – when buying sets of Dickens in the improbable hope of reading them – mere self-deceivers. In 'England Your England' he denounces the left-wing English intelligentsia for being 'generally negative' and 'querulous': adjectives which, from this distance, seem to fit Orwell pretty aptly. Given that he died at the age of forty-six, it's scary to imagine the crustiness that might have set in had he reached pensionable age.

Nowhere is he more dogmatic than in his attitude to writing: what it is for, how it should be done, and who does it badly. Auden is 'pure scoutmaster'; Carlyle 'with all his cleverness . . . had not even the wit to write plain, straightforward English'; Rupert Brooke's 'Grantchester' is 'accumulated vomit'. Even those he approves of have major faults: Dickens is really 'rather ignorant' about how life works; H. G. Wells is 'too sane to understand the modern world'; while Orwell's 'defence' of Kipling is oddly patronising. There are huge generalisations about how writers develop and age; and for all his moral clarity about totalitarian language, his own prescriptiveness is sometimes severe, sometimes woolly. 'All art is to some extent propaganda' looks striking, but is greatly weakened by the 'to some extent', and what, finally, does it mean? Only that all art is 'about' something, even if it is only about itself. 'Art for Art's sake' – a concept Orwell would abhor – is just 'propaganda' for Art itself, which the movement was well aware of. Then there is: 'A novelist who simply disregards the major public events of the moment is generally either a footler or a plain idiot.' Since this dismisses both novelists of the private life and those who (as was common in the nineteenth century) set their stories a generation or two back, out go Austen, the Brontës, Flaubert, James and so on, and so on.

'Good prose is like a windowpane.' As an instruction to cub reporters and old hacks – also as a self-instruction of the kind writer-critics issue to the world while actually describing their own procedures – it sounds reasonable enough. But it begs questions, as does Orwell's other key instruction, from 'Politics and the English Language': 'Let the meaning choose the word, and not the other way round.' Together, these dicta presuppose, and instruct, that writing is a matter of examining the world, reflecting upon it, deducing what you want to say, putting that meaning or message into words whose transparency allows the reader, now gazing through the same windowpane from the same position, to see the world exactly as you have seen it. But does anyone, even Orwell, actually write like that? And are words glass? Most writing comes from an inchoate process; ideas may indeed propose words, but sometimes words propose ideas (or both transactions occur within the same sentence). As E. M. Forster, a frequent target of Orwell's, put it (or rather, quoted), in *Aspects of the Novel*: 'How do I tell what I think till I see what I say?' To Orwell this might seem a piece of pansy-left whimsy; but it probably accords more closely to the experience of many writers.

In *Down and Out in Paris and London*, Orwell enumerated the things about England that made him glad to be home: 'bathrooms, armchairs, mint sauce, new potatoes properly cooked, brown bread, marmalade, beer made with veritable hops'. In 'England Your England' he celebrated 'a nation of stamp-collectors, pigeon-fanciers, amateur carpenters, coupon-snippers, darts-players, crossword-puzzle fans'. In 1993, the Trollope-loving prime minister John Major, with his party split, the currency on the slide and his own authority diminishing, found similar refuge in those seemingly eternal aspects of Englishness:

> Fifty years from now, Britain will still be the country of long shadows on cricket grounds, warm beer, invincible green suburbs, dog lovers and pools fillers, and, as George Orwell said, 'Old maids bicycling to holy communion through the morning mist', and, if we get our way, Shakespeare will still be read even in school.

Less than a third of those fifty years have elapsed, but many pools fillers now play the National Lottery or log on to Internet gambling sites; global warming is giving the English a taste for chilled beer; while the bicycling Anglicans are being replaced by Muslims driving to the suburban mosque. All prophets risk posthumous censure, even mockery; and the Orwell we celebrate nowadays is less the predictor than the social and political analyst. Those of us born in the immediate post-war years grew up with the constant half-expectation that 1984 would bring all the novel described: immovable geopolitical blocs, plus brutal state surveillance and control. Today, the English may have their sluggardly couch-potato side; their liberties have been somewhat diminished, and they are recorded by CCTV cameras more often than any other nation on earth. But otherwise 1984 passed with a sigh of relief, while 1989 brought a louder one.

Orwell believed in 1936 that 'the combines can never squeeze the small independent bookseller out of existence as they have squeezed the grocer and the milkman'. That 'never' was a risky call. And on a larger scale, he believed throughout

the Second World War that peace would bring the British
revolution he desired, with 'blood in the gutters' and the 'red
militias billeted in the Ritz', as he put in private diary and
public essay. And after the revolution:

> The Stock Exchange will be pulled down, the horse
> plough will give way to the tractor, the country houses
> will be turned into children's holiday camps, the Eton
> and Harrow match will be forgotten . . .

One out of four on the vision thing; and tractors were hardly
a difficult pick.

Against such a background, it would be rash to try to
predict the continuing afterlife of Orwell's work. Many of his
phrases and mental tropes have already sunk into the conscious
and unconscious mind, and we carry them with us as we
carry Freudian tropes, whether or not we have read Freud.
Some of those English couch potatoes watch programmes
called *Big Brother* and *Room 101*. And if we allow ourselves to
hope for a future in which all of Orwell's warnings have been
successfully heeded, and in which *Animal Farm* has become
as archaic a text as *Rasselas*, the world will have to work its
way through a lot of dictators and repressive systems first. In
Burma there is a joke that Orwell wrote not just a single
novel about the country, but a trilogy: *Burmese Days*, *Animal
Farm* and *Nineteen Eighty-Four*.

Orwell shared with Dickens a hatred of tyranny, and in
his essay on the Victorian novelist distinguished two types of
revolutionary. On the one hand there are change-of-heart
people, who believe that if you improve human nature, all the
problems of society will fall away; and on the other social
engineers, who believe that once you fix society – make it
fairer, more democratic, less divided – then the problems of
human nature will fall away. These two approaches 'appeal to
different individuals, and they probably show a tendency to

alternate in point of time'. Dickens was a change-of-heart man, Orwell a systems-and-structures man, not least because he thought human beings recidivist, and beyond mere self-help. 'The central problem – how to prevent power from being abused – remains unresolved.' And until then, it is safe to predict that Orwell will remain a living writer.

FORD'S *THE GOOD SOLDIER*

THE BACK COVER of the 1950s Vintage edition of *The Good Soldier* always made poignant reading. 'Fifteen distinguished critics' had been assembled to puff Ford Madox Ford's novel of 1915. They had all subscribed to a single statement: 'Ford's *The Good Soldier* is one of the fifteen or twenty greatest novels produced in English in our century.' And then the names, including Leon Edel and Allen Tate, Graham Greene and John Crowe Ransom, William Carlos Williams and Jean Stafford.

There was something both heroic and hopeless about this, as there was much that was heroic and hopeless about Ford himself. Fifteen critics ought to be better than five, but somehow the number overpleads. 'One of the fifteen or twenty greatest novels' sounds as if it can't make up its mind – again, a very Fordian vacillation, but one that weakens rather than strengthens the claim: ah, so Joseph Henry Jackson thinks it's in the top fifteen, but Willard Thorp only ranks it in the top twenty? As for 'in our century' – that seemed rather presumptuous with four more decades of it still to run.

Yet the statement remains poignant because you can hear the literary virtue behind it: look, *we know* this guy is good, so will you please, *please* read him? Ford has never lacked supporters, but he has always lacked readers. In 1929 Hugh Walpole wrote that 'there is no greater literary neglect of our time in England than the novels and poems of Ford'. To which Ford replied, 'It is just that the public *will* not read me.'

Trying to explain it further – to himself, as much as to

his correspondent Gerald Bullett – he wrote from Toulon in
1933:

> Why should a London public like my works? My
> constatations of life have dubious international back-
> grounds; they contain nothing about British birds'
> nests, wild-flowers or rock gardens; they are 'machined'
> with a Franco-American modernity that must be dis-
> agreeable indeed to the inhabitants of, say, Cheltenham.
> To them, on account of the 'time-shift' and projection
> instead of description, they must be quite incompre-
> hensible and inexpressibly boring. Between the Middle
> West and the Eastern sea-board of the United States
> as well as round the Pantheon where those devices
> saw light they are already regarded as *vieux jeu*, accepted
> as classics which you must know of, and used for
> Manuals in University English Classes. So I go on
> writing in the hope that, a hundred and fifty years
> from today, what I turn out may be used as an alter-
> native study in, say, Durham University. And at any
> rate, I have the comfortable feeling that none of our
> entrants for the Davis Cup will have been kept off
> the playing fields of Eton by a reprehensible engross-
> ment in my novels.

Ford sees the problem as purely internal, textual; yet there
are many external – and overlapping – reasons for his past
and continuing neglect. He presents no usefully crisp literary
profile; he wrote far too much, and in too many genres; he
fails to fit easily into university courses. He seems to fall down
a hole between late Victorianism and modernism, between a
childhood of being dandled by Liszt and seeing Swinburne
gambol, and a subsequent career as the avuncular facilitator
of Pound, Hemingway and Lawrence. He also presented himself
as an elderly party fading out before this new generation,

which was probably a bad tactical move. If ambitious novelists should all study *The Good Soldier* as an example of the possibilities of narrative (how dull that makes it sound), they would also do well to look at Ford's life as a prime example of negative career management.

He had the sort of large, soft, bonhomous presence which provoked attack, and also a suffering gentlemanliness which declined to reply (this naturally provoked renewed attack). He quarrelled endlessly with publishers, regarding them as tradesmen, and impertinent for wanting to read his manuscripts before buying them. Even those who admired Ford were often irritated by him. Rebecca West said that being embraced by Ford was 'like being the toast under a poached egg'. Robert Lowell's praise of the 'master, mammoth mumbler' is lapped with fondish mockery:

> . . . *tell me why*
> *The bales of your left-over novels buy*
> *Less than a bandage for your gouty foot.*
> *Wheel-horse, O unforgetting elephant . . .*

Those who weren't fond of Ford were more than irritated. Hemingway – whom Ford had made the mistake of promoting – denounced him to Stein and Toklas as 'an absolute liar and crook always motivated by the finest synthetic English gentility'. Once, when he was near Philadelphia, Ford applied to see the Barnes collection. Admittedly (if characteristically), he made his approach through the wrong person; but tactical maladroitness alone can't account for the ferocity of Dr Barnes's telegram from Geneva: 'Would rather burn my collection than let Ford Madox Ford see it'.

He changed his name, from Hueffer to Ford; he changed his country of domicile more than once; he was sometimes more ambitious for literature than for himself. Even so, it is strange how completely he fails to blip on certain radar screens.

Edmund Wilson scarcely mentions him in his journals and criticism: did he simply miss (or miss the point of) *Parade's End*, despite sharing the war with Ford? Virginia Woolf and Orwell are silent. Waugh never mentions him in letters, journals or criticism: this seems even more peculiar than Wilson's case. Like Ford, Waugh wrote a book about Rossetti; while his Second World War trilogy, *Sword of Honour*, seems manifestly related to Ford's First World War quartet, in its setting of marital warfare against the wider landscape of the real thing, and its pitting of a vindictive, pursuing wife against an out-of-his-time gentlemanly husband.

With Ford, even praise somehow turned itself to his disadvantage. In his preface to a 1927 reissue of *The Good Soldier*, he recounts the story of an admirer telling him it was 'the finest novel in the English language'. To which Ford's friend John Roker rejoined, 'Ah, yes, it is. But you have left a word out. It is the finest French novel in the English language.' In a tauter, less authentic form – 'the best French novel in the language' – this is often cited, famously in Lowell's *Life Studies*. If readers can be put off by titles (I resisted *The Catcher in the Rye* for many years, imagining it to be a prairie baseball novel), so they can by hyping tags. What's the point of writing a French novel in English? you might roughly ask. That's a pretty fey thing to do, isn't it? And not exactly entering a competitive field either: what's the second-best French novel in the language?

France certainly provided *The Good Soldier*'s point of emulative origin: 'I had in those days an ambition', wrote Ford subsequently, 'that was to do for the English novel what in *Fort comme la mort*, Maupassant had done for the French.' What Maupassant did was this: into a novel which for much of its length appears to be a kind of tranced, Degasian treatment of the society woman in late-nineteenth-century Paris, delighting in the *douces petites gourmandises* of feminine existence among *la fine fleur du high-life*, he gradually introduces the theme of violently transgressive passion – that of a society painter for the daughter of his long-term mistress. The painter's tragedy – if that's what it is – springs from the flaying difference between the easy love of youth and the desperate (the more desperate because unwanted and unrequited) love of age. 'It's the fault of our hearts for not growing old,' laments the hero-victim, whose emotionally incestuous love moves the final quarter of the novel to a pitch of terror and a heightened, operatic mode. The love that dares not speak its existence finally prefers death to acknowledgement.

Ford applies these tropes and torments to a very English set of characters (even the Americans are such Anglophiles that their Americanness barely registers) from a similar leisured class. But *The Good Soldier* is much less of a social novel than *Fort comme la mort*. The progressive disintegration of Edward Ashburnham, good soldier and seemingly model Englishman, takes place in festering privacy: initially among a tight Racinian quartet of expatriates at the German spa of Nauheim; ultimately with Ashburnham's ward Nancy Rufford. His relationship with her is plainly – as in the Maupassant – emotionally incestuous, and may well be more than this: Ford's biographer Max Saunders has made a persuasive case for Nancy being Ashburnham's daughter. In terms of emotional heat *The Good Soldier* is even Frencher than *Fort comme la mort*. Maupassant turns up the burners only towards the end of his novel. Ford raises the stakes in both madness and terror (and body count); but his greatest audacity is to start at the highest emotional pitch, and then keep raising it.

Cyril Connolly in *The Modern Movement* praised *The Good Soldier* with rather idle words about its 'energy and intelligence'. Looked at now, the novel barges its way into the modernist club for very different reasons: its immaculate use of a ditheringly unreliable narrator, its sophisticated disguise of true narrative behind a false facade of apparent narrative, its self-reflectingness, its deep duality about human motive, intention and experience, and its sheer boldness as a project. Greene wrote in 1962: 'I don't know how many times in nearly forty years I have come back to this novel of Ford's, every time to discover a new aspect to admire.'

Take the novel's famous opening sentence, one of high plangency and enormous claim: 'This is the saddest story I have ever heard.' The first part of the sentence takes our attention and rightly so. It cannot logically be until the second reading (and it may not be until the third or fourth) that we note the falsity of the final word. Because it's not a story Dowell, the narrator, has 'heard'. It's one in which he has participated, has been right up to the neck, heart and guts in; he's the one telling it, we're the ones hearing it. He says 'heard' instead of 'told' because he's affecting distance from his 'tale of passion', declining to admit complicity. And if the second verb of the first sentence of the book is unreliable – if it gives a creak under the foot as we put our weight on it – then we must be prepared to treat every line as warily; we must prowl soft-footed through the text, alive for every board's moan and plaint.

This is a novel about the human heart. It says so on the first page. Yet the word is set differently in its first two appearances, once plainly, once between quotes. When is a heart not a heart? When it's a medical condition, a 'heart'. Ford plays for a while with this separation of meaning. We might expect that having a 'heart' means that affairs of the heart are off-limits. But this is a false facade: it seems that the two characters who are at Nauheim for medical purposes – Florence Dowell and Edward Ashburnham himself – are the very two who are indulging their unquote-marked hearts; whereas the two healthy onlookers, Dowell and Leonora Ashburnham, are the two with a different sort of heart trouble – hearts which are cold or killed. However, this paradox turns out to be a second false facade: Florence's 'heart' is a fake, a got-up condition to keep her husband out of her bedroom; while later on we learn (or seem to learn – there is a lot of seeming to learn in this novel) that Ashburnham doesn't have a 'heart' either: the Ashburnhams are in Nauheim because of Maisie Maidan, whom they have brought to the spa from India for treatment. She – Maisie – is (or seems to be) the only character in the novel who has a heart in both the amatory and medical senses of the word. Not surprisingly, she is soon to die.

So the novel's language shows its strategy. It plays with the reader as it reveals and conceals truth. And part of Ford's great achievement is to find the perfect voice for paradoxical narrative. In Dowell he gives us a bluff, know-nothing narrator, who forgets to tell us his Christian name until the book is nearly over, and seems in his bumbling way to have wrecked his own story by giving away its outcome on page two. Ford uses an armchair bore to tell a story of great subtlety; also one of deep emotional cruelty and pain. He deploys the natural tropes and forgettings of a bad narrator to enrich the narrative, delay our understanding, and finally to deliver us the whole (or whole-ish) picture: in other words, he makes good narrative out of bad.

Ford also plays relentlessly on the reader's desire to trust the narrator. We want – or want to want – to believe what we are told, and dummy-like we fall into every pit dug for us. Even when we know we can't trust Dowell, we carry on doing so, to our cost. This trustingness before narrative recidivism has its counterpart within the novel, in Leonora's trustingness before Ashburnham's sexual recidivism. Of course, it is our own 'fault' as readers: the hazard warnings are plain enough. 'My wife and I knew Captain and Mrs Ashburnham as well as it is possible to know anybody, and yet, in another sense, we knew nothing at all about them.' 'Was that last remark of hers the remark of a harlot, or is it what every decent woman . . . thinks at the bottom of her heart?' 'Is all this digression or isn't it digression?' Such items from the opening pages are more than indicators of Dowell's candid indecisiveness. They establish the switchback rhythm of the whole book; they set up the pulse, the paradox and the dualism of the story.

Listening to Dowell is like coming upon a hysteric who insists that everything is normal and he himself is fine, thank you very much. He goes backwards, forwards, sideways, switching times and tenses. He even comes up with an 'impossible tense', beginning a sentence like this: 'Supposing that you should come upon us sitting together . . .' – as if such a coming-upon were still possible. Yet he has already explained that two of the central quartet are dead, and as if suddenly realising that himself, he readjusts, and the sentence resolves itself in a 'possible tense', the past conditional: '. . . you would have said that as human affairs go, we were an extraordinarily safe castle'. Time and again a seemingly ordinary sentence will have contradicted itself by its end; there are sentences beginning 'And' which appear to supply continuation from the previous sentence, but in fact give a denial to it; there are false abuttings and leaky grammatical joints.

So the prose's dividedness points us directly to the towering either/ors of the story: Ashburnham as good soldier or plundering shit; Leonora as marital martyr or vengeful destroyer; the narrator as honest misprisioner or complicit evader, timid domestic dormouse or repressed homoerotic swooner over Edward Ashburnham; and so on. There is the wider dividedness between social face and inner urging; between emotional expectation and emotional reality; between Protestant and Catholic (this last aspect seems rather underworked: it's as if the Catholic element is mainly introduced to produce women of exceptional innocence and marital adhesiveness – and thus up the ante when they face the complexities and wiles of sex). Beyond this, the dividedness of the personality between the conscious and the unconscious mind. And beyond all this, the realisation that the answer to either/or may not be one or the other – is Ashburnham a deep sentimentalist, as Dowell constantly, indeed infuriatingly, insists, or a ruthless sexual predator? – but both. At the end of the novel, Nancy Rufford briefly emerges from deep madness to utter the word 'shuttle-cocks', which we understand as a brief lucid memory of how she has been treated by the Ashburnhams. It is also the way the reader has been treated, soaring high between opposing bashes.

Ford's masterpiece is a novel which constantly asks how to tell a story, which pretends to fail at narrative while richly succeeding. It also openly doubts what we easily think of as character. 'For who in this world can give anyone a character,' Dowell asks at one point of Ashburnham (typically, there is a creak of the floorboard here as well: 'give someone a character' can mean 'describe', but also 'give the social thumbs-up to'). Dowell's answer to his own question is: 'I don't mean to say that one cannot form an average estimate of the way a person will behave. But one cannot be certain of the way any man will behave in every case – and until one can do that a "character" is of no use to anyone.' Ford later refined this line in his novel *The New Humpty-Dumpty*, where it comes from the Duke of Kintyre's mouth: '"Any man," he said slowly, "is any sort of man, some time or another, you know."' Ford's approach is to get at character – and, more widely, truth – not just indirectly or contradictingly, but often by way of ignorance.

Some years ago, while writing about Ford, I ran into one of our better-known literary novelists, whose use of indirection and the bumbling narrator seemed to me to derive absolutely from Ford. I mentioned this (a little more tactfully than I have stated it here), and asked if he had read Ford. Yes, indeed he had. Would he mind if I mentioned this fact in my piece? There was a pause (actually a couple of days) before the reply: 'Please pretend I haven't read *The Good Soldier*. I'd prefer it that way.'

More recently, I was talking to my friend Ian McEwan, who told me that a few years ago he'd been staying in a house with a well-stocked library. There he found a copy of *The Good Soldier*, which he read and admired greatly. A while later, he wrote *On Chesil Beach*, that brilliant novella in which passion, and Englishness and misunderstanding, lead to emotional catastrophe. Only after publishing the book did he realise that he had unconsciously given his two main characters the names Edward (as in Ashburnham) and Florence (as in Dowell). He is quite happy for me to pass this on.

So Ford's presences, and subterranean influence, continue. I am not sure whether calling a novelist 'undervalued' helps or not. Perhaps it would do more good just to assume and assert Ford's value. He is not so much a writer's writer (which can suggest hermeticism) as a proper reader's writer. *The Good Soldier* needs The Good Reader.

FORD AND PROVENCE

MOST FRANCOPHILES, BESIDE their general attachment to French customs and culture, have an additional fondness for a particular region or city: for
landscapists it might be Burgundy, for monument-sniffers the
Loire, for solitarists and hikers the Massif Central. Those who
want to be reminded of a certain kind of England go for the
Dordogne, where the *Daily Mail* is readily available. Many
simply choose Paris, which might seem to sum everything up,
and where – unlike in London – most people still have regional
attachments as strong as their metropolitan ones. Ford Madox
Ford lived in Paris off and on throughout the 1920s – editing
the *Transatlantic Review*, living with the Australian painter Stella
Bowen, having his affair with Jean Rhys, knowing Pound and
Joyce and Hemingway and Fitzgerald, having the young Basil
Bunting as his office boy. He enjoyed a full literary and social
life in the (largely non-French) bohemia of Montparnasse. He
once went up in a lift with Jean Rhys and James Joyce; despite
his poor eyesight, Joyce managed to notice that Rhys's dress
was undone at the back, and hooked her up. And yet Ford,
who wrote a book called *New York is Not America*, also knew
that Paris is Not France. For him the real France was a region
which official 'France' – northern, bureaucratic, centralising
– had long ago conquered and attempted to both dismantle
and dis-language: Provence.

His passionate attachment to the region came from his
father, Francis Hueffer, music critic of *The Times*, who published
a book on the Troubadours, and wrote Provençal poetry.

Hueffer knew Frédéric Mistral (1830–1914), the poet at the heart of the revival of Provençal, who in 1854 had set up the Félibrige with seven fellow poets, and an academy to codify the language (the result being the great dictionary known as *Trésor du Félibrige*). According to Ford, his father played chess with Mistral and was received into the Félibrige. According to Ford, the only two things his father taught him were 'a very little Provençal' and rudimentary chess. The phrase 'according to Ford' needs tacitly applying to much he wrote of an autobiographical nature (and there were eight such volumes), since he had a great contempt for fact and a counter-vailing belief in the 'absolute accuracy' of impressions. His lies grew perhaps ever more extravagant with time. According to Ford, the great chef Escoffier once said to him, 'I could learn cooking from you', while Henry James came to him, with tears in his eyes, asking for help with a plot. In *A Mirror to France* (1926), Ford explains how he had attended Dreyfus's second trial at Rennes in 1899, and that 'it was in the changing lights and shadows of that courthouse' that he first 'began to have a sense of the profound cleavage that was to come between opposing schools of French thought'. In fact, all that time he was busy on the Kentish coast collaborating with Conrad (nor is it remotely plausible that a French military court would have allowed him to be present). Faced with Ford's multitudinous fabrications, his biographer Max Saunders rightly concludes that it is a question of 'asking less whether what Ford says is *true*, and more what it *means*'.

Ford's love of Provence can, however, be accorded the status of both a major fact and a lifelong impression. For some years he and Stella Bowen would head south by the overnight train from the Gare de Lyon. The rich and fashionable (including Florence Dowell in *The Good Soldier*) would take the famous Train Bleu, a privately run, first-class-only oper-ation, whose passengers might dine beforehand at the restaurant of the same name, high overlooking the tracks, for a long time the ritziest station brasserie in the world. Ford and Bowen would travel second class on the humbler 9.40. Nowadays the TGV from the Gare de Lyon will get you to Avignon in just over two and a half hours; then the city was reached after ten and a half hours, at about eight in the morning, with the 'urgent muddy Rhône' beside you and the first streaks of light in the sky. But there are advantages to slow travel, to the sense of changing landscape, to dozing off, and waking up, as Bowen put it, 'amongst the pale olives, the dark cypresses, the grey rocks and the flat-roofed, flat-faced houses which in spite of their poverty and austerity seem to hold promise of a sweeter life within their dry old walls'.

Quite where Provence began was another of Ford's variable facts. Sometimes he said it was at Lyon, at other times Valence or Montélimar. Perhaps it depended on when the train jogged him awake. The shape of it was always a triangle, with the Rhône wandering down the middle: a narrow one like a slice of Brie if Provence began at Lyon, a fatter, more equilateral one if it began lower down. The Rhône also divided what Ford thought of as the 'true Provence' of the east bank – where are found the three A-list cities of Arles, Avignon and Aix, plus Ford's favourite town of Tarascon – from 'the sort of quasi-Provence that contains Montpellier, Béziers, Carcassonne and Perpignan' on the other side. This reflects the old division between the Empire or east bank and the Royaume or west. Thus, according to Ford, the most famous southern writer of the nineteenth century, Alphonse Daudet, 'was not a true Provençal', since he came from Nîmes, which 'with all its charms' – the Maison Carré, the bullfights, and 'one memorable eating place' – 'is not true Provence'.

Ford and Bowen were first invited south to stay in the 'magical' yet at the same time 'quite ordinary little villa' of Harold Monro, founder of the Poetry Bookshop, in the winter of 1922–3. Next they tried Tarascon, from where he wrote

'Life is so relatively cheap in France . . . that I shouldn't
wonder if we settled down here for good. Besides, the French
make much of me – which at my age is inspiring.' After a
brief diversion into the wilder Ardèche, the Spanish Cubist
Juan Gris and his wife Josette suggested Toulon, then as now
a navy town, and therefore cheap. Bowen and Ford were
similar, according to Stella, in that each was 'a rolling stone
with domestic instincts and a steady longing for a house, a
garden and a view'. If they found this anywhere, they did so
at Cap Brun outside Toulon, where they spent two winters,
and whither Ford returned with Bowen's successor after they
had parted company. In her admirably sane, generous and
un-Fordianly trustworthy memoir, *Drawn from Life*, Bowen
analyses the spell Provence cast on them:

> It is something to do with the light, I suppose, and
> the airiness and bareness and frugality of life in the
> Midi which induces a simplicity of thought, and a
> kind of whittling to the bone whatever may be the
> matter in hand. Sunlight reflected from red tiled floors
> on to whitewashed walls, closed shutters and open
> windows and an air so soft that you live equally in
> and out of doors, suggest an experience so sweetly
> simple that you wonder that life ever appeared the
> tangled, hustling and distracting piece of nonsense you
> once thought it. Your mind relaxes, your thoughts
> spread out and take their shape, phobias disappear, and
> if passions become quicker, they also lose their power
> of deadly strangulation. Reason wins. And you are
> released from the necessity of owning things. There is
> no need to be cosy. A pot of flowers, a strip of fabric
> on the wall, and your room is furnished. Your comforts
> are the light and warmth provided by nature, and your
> ornaments are the orange trees outside.

Life was cheap, and the more so because Ford was an enthusiastic kitchen gardener. He claimed to have studied under the great Professor Gressent in Paris, which is deeply improbable; though he at least read him, learning that 'three hoeings are worth two coatings of dung'. But he combined science with superstition, never planting on a Friday or a 13th, but always on a 9th, an 18th or a 27th, and sowing seed only when the moon was waxing. He cultivated those Mediterranean items – aubergines, garlic, peppers – later introduced to the British by Elizabeth David. Bowen attests to Ford's culinary skills, even if he 'reduced the kitchen to the completest chaos'. He also took to the local wine. The delicate Gris said, 'He absorbs a terrifying quantity of alcohol. I never thought one could drink so much.' (Ford, who was a great layer-down of the law, assured James Joyce in a letter that 'The primary responsibility of a wine is to be red.') Meanwhile, Bowen discovered a small shop in Toulon selling nothing but different kinds of olive oil, to be tasted from a row of taps on a piece of bread – this at a time when the British were still pouring the stuff not into their mouths but into their waxed-up ears. And Ford liked the way he was treated in France simply for being a writer. Bowen describes the pleasure he felt on receiving a letter which began 'Cher et illustre Maître'. According to Ford, when they moved into their house in Toulon, their landlord, a retired naval quarter-master, was so delighted to have a poet for a tenant that he drove a hundred and fifty miles to fetch him a root of asphodel – because asphodels grew on the Elysian Fields, and every poet must have 'that fabulous herb' in his garden. If only Ford hadn't specified 'a hundred and fifty miles', we might be more inclined to believe him.

'There are in this world only two earthly Paradises . . . Provence . . . and the Reading Room of the British Museum.' Provence was not only itself, but also the absence of the North, where most human vices accumulated. The North meant

aggression, the Gothic, the 'sadically mad cruelties of the
Northern Middle Ages' and the 'Northern tortures of ennui
and indigestion'. Ford was a great believer in diet and digestion as controllers of human behaviour (Conrad agreed, main-
taining that the 'ill-cooked food' of Native Americans caused
'raging dyspepsia' and hence their 'unreasonable violence').
South good, North bad: Ford was convinced that no one
could be 'completely whole either physically or mentally'
without 'a reasonable amount of garlic' in their diet, and
equally obsessed with the malign effect of Brussels sprouts,
an item of particular northern mischief. Provence was a place
of good thoughts and moral actions, 'for there the apple will
not flourish and the Brussels sprout will not grow at all'. The
North was also full of excessive meat-eating, which caused
not just indigestion but lunacy: 'Any alienist will tell you that
the first thing he does with a homicidal maniac after he gets
him into an asylum is to deliver, with immense purges, his
stomach from bull-beef and Brussels sprouts.' Another of Ford's
charmingly bonkers theories was about the grapefruit. The
English translators of the Bible had been misguided in writing
that Eve was tempted by an apple. The word they should
have been aiming for was shaddock, another name for the
grapefruit. Now, in Provence grapefruit grow abundantly, but
are scorned by the inhabitants, who might occasionally use
a little of the zest in cooking, but would routinely throw the
fruit to the pigs. Since Provençals have never eaten of the
grapefruit, therefore they have never fallen, therefore they live
in Paradise, QED.

But Provence meant far more to Ford than easy living
and sound diet; beneath its surface pleasures lay a mythic
and historical substructure. Provence was where the Great
Trade Route, having run from China across Asia and Asia
Minor to Venice and Genoa and along the north shore of
the Mediterranean, finally turned north at Marseilles. Then
it went 'up the Rhône . . . inland, by way of Beaucaire and

Lyons to Paris; then down the Seine past Rouen to the
English Channel which it crossed at its narrowest and so
away along the South Coast of England past Ottery St Mary's
to the Scilly Isles where it ended abruptly'. It brought the
flow of civilisation with it – or, at least, the display goods
of civilisation – and, for Ford, 'Provence is the only region
on the Great Trade Route fit for the habitation of a proper
man.' Of all the towns and cities he loved Tarascon 'the best
in the world'; it was where Good King René held his court,
and where, according to Ford, you couldn't sleep for the
noise of the nightingales. King René also had a court at
Aix-en-Provence, but Ford didn't like the city – 'birthplace
of Cézanne though it be, and though it be the gravest and
most stately eighteenth-century town that you will find
anywhere'. The problem was that Aix contained the Parlement, the intermediary through which successive French
kings ruled: from there 'the lawyers of the Parlement . . .
fixed on Provence the gadfly yoke of armies of functionaries
that have ever since bled and crippled not Provence alone
but all the country of the Lilies'.

What does civilisation, as embodied by Provence, consist
of? In *A Mirror to France* Ford gave his answer:

> Chivalric generosity, frugality, pure thought and the arts
> are the first requisites of a Civilisation – and the only
> requisites of a Civilisation; and such traces of chivalric
> generosity, frugality, pure thought and the arts as our
> prewar, European civilisation of white races could
> exhibit came to us from the district of Southern France
> on the shores of the Mediterranean where flourished
> the Counts of Toulouse, olive trees, the mistral, the
> Romance Tradition, Bertran de Born, the Courts of
> Love, and the only really amiable Heresy of which I
> know.

The period covered runs roughly from the twelfth to the fifteenth century. The 'amiable' heresy was Albigensianism, whose piety and virtue (and Manichean doctrine) brought its destruction in a papal crusade led with immense cruelty by the English Simon de Montfort in 1209–13. The Troubadours – of whom Bertran de Born (*c.*1140–*c.*1215) was one of the most famous – and their Courts of Love continued up to the end of the thirteenth century, though their influence was much curtailed when Provence west of the Rhône was ceded to Louis XI in 1229. Avignon prospered between 1309 and 1408 as the seat of seven popes and two anti-popes, while Good King René (1408–80) presided over the final efflorescence of Provençal culture, after which the region east of the Rhône was in turn ceded to the French king. This whole period came in later centuries to represent a kind of Merrie France – tournaments, chivalry and courtly love, with wise rulers overseeing peace and human contentment. According to Ford, the first piece of French literature he read as a schoolboy was a rapturous description by Daudet of life in Avignon under the popes: processions, pilgrimages, streets strewn with flowers, the sound of bells at all hours, 'the tic-tac of the lace bobbins, and the rustle of the shuttles weaving the cloth of the gold chasubles, the little hammers of the goldsmiths tapping the altar-cruets' and 'the undersound of tambourines coming from the Bridge'. Daudet continued:

> For, in our country, when the people is glad, there must be dancing, there must be . . . dancing! And since, in those days, the streets of the city were too narrow for the *farandole*, fifes and tambourines kept to the Bridge of Avignon, in the fresh breezes of the Rhône and day and night was dancing; was . . . dancing! Ah, happy days, happy city! The pikes that did not cut; the state prisons where wine lay cooling! Never

famine, never wars . . . That was how the Popes of
the Comtat knew how to govern their people; that
is why their people has so much regretted them!

Ford is more idiosyncratic and textured than Daudet in
his appreciation of the South. Provence was not just a lost
golden land; despite conquest, it was both tenacious and inva-
sive. The extermination of the language had been decreed
under Louis XI, François I and Louis XIV, but Provençal
continued to be spoken for centuries, and was there waiting
to be revived and made official once again by the Félibrige.
And though France was 'the first Mass Product in the way of
modern nations', Provence, despite being crushed and
subsumed, had the revenge of the defeated: it infiltrated the
dominant culture. The virtues and values of Provence spread
up through the remnants of the Great Trade Route, so that
France was civilised to the extent that she submitted to this
reverse takeover. And Provence was not just a region but also
a state of mind – indulgent, fantastical, credulous – and this
element fed into those harsh and pragmatic owners up in the
North.

Ford's historical and travel writing is vivid, often tenden-
tious, and always personal. His nostalgia becomes blatantly
solipsistic, for instance, when he looks at the rewards and
public standing of the Troubadour poets. He himself was
perpetually impoverished: in 1907 he set what must be some
kind of record by publishing six books while also applying to
the Royal Literary Fund for financial assistance. How different
it was back in the twelfth century:

The Troubadour appears as taking the place of the
Hollywood star – but of the Hollywood star who
should not be only performer but the extraordinarily
skilful author and composer of the piece . . . As writer
and performer Peire Vidal was the equal of the highest

in the land and the terror of noble husbands though
but the son of small tradespeople.

This was a key feature of Troubadour art for Ford: it was
'essentially both democratic and aristocratic'. By which he
meant that the Troubadours might be of humble origin and
yet address their love songs to aristocratic women. But he also
meant that this was how all the arts should be: 'democratic'
inasmuch as anyone could make them, and anyone could enjoy
them; but the process was 'aristocratic' in the sense of being
highly skilled, difficult and rare.

Ford described himself as a 'sentimental Tory' who liked
'pomp, banners, divine rights, unreasonable ceremonies and
ceremoniousness'. He presented himself as a rather old-
fashioned English officer and gentleman. His grandfather had
'insisted characteristically that although one must know
French with accuracy one must speak it with a marked
English accent to show that one is an English gentleman. I
still do.' (But this being Ford, there is a contradictory explan-
ation provided by Stella Bowen: his French sounded English
because he never moved his lips enough.) The honourable,
chivalric man, trying to do his best in a modern world which
fails to recognise his virtues, is a recurrent figure in Ford's
work. And there is a quietly insistent chivalric element underlying *The Good Soldier*. The two couples at the heart of this
story of destructive passion meet for the first time in the
hotel restaurant of a German spa town. They find a table to
suit them; it is round; Florence Dowell comments, 'And so
the whole round table is begun'— quoting Malory. She and
her husband have visited Provence, 'where even the saddest
stories are gay'; and Dowell, the narrator, at one point tells,
in his prosy, non-understanding way, the story of Peire Vidal.
The Good Soldier of the title, Edward Ashburnham, is
presented as an absolute English gentleman forever on a
'feudal' quest to help others; his ward, Nancy Rufford, who

is in love with him, specifically links him to three chivalric figures of different cultures – Lohengrin, the Chevalier Bayard and El Cid. Dowell, who is in love with Nancy, explains himself with the novel's famous, high-Romantic line, 'I just wanted to marry her as some people want to go to Carcassonne.' And at the end of the book, after the great emotional 'smash' is over, Dowell revisits Provence: 'I have seen again for a glimpse, from a swift train, Beaucaire with the beautiful white tower, Tarascon with the square castle, the great Rhône, the immense stretches of the Crau. I have rushed through all Provence – and all Provence no longer matters.'

It no longer matters because its high-hearted truths have been shown to be deluded. Ford may have loved Provence and its golden mythology, but he was also a modern novelist, guided by the emotional truthfulness of Flaubert and Maupassant. He knew that 'the saddest stories' nowadays are rarely gay, but just very sad, if not murderously violent; and that any gaiety around is likely to come from misunderstanding and self-deception. He knew also that the human heart is 'defective'. For all his convincing self-presentation as a moth-eaten old gent – E. M. Forster snootily called him 'a fly-blown man of letters', Paul Nash 'Silenus in tweeds' – Ford understood the modern world, and the new reality that opposed the past's lingering myths. After all, in 1913, two years before *The Good Soldier* was published, he had visited the totemic city of Carcassonne, towards which Dowell and others feel such a romantic impulsion. And what had Ford discovered there? Snow and rabies.

Ford's Provence was an ideal lost world, a cradle of civilisation, and a reference point in his fiction. But the region contained more than just the past and present; it also suggested a possible future. In *Provence* (1935) Ford at one point asks to be regarded not as a moralist or historian, but 'simply as prophet'. Civilisation is 'staggering to its end' and he wants to show 'what will happen to it if it does not take Provence of the XIII century for its model'. Ford had seen service as a transport officer in the First World War, where he was gassed; and he spent his last twenty years (before his death in 1939) watching the grim chest-beating of nations and ideologies across Europe. He loathed empty-headed nationalism, violence, transnational standardisation, mechanisation, and most of the doings of financiers. He was also a writer, and thus a citizen not of any one country but of the world; and he wondered how that world might emerge from the great smash that was coming, and avoid further smashes. How might the human brute be tamed? Not by bigger groupings, by signing up to yet more overarching -ologies, by exterminating languages and individualisms. Perhaps, he thought, we should become local again, live in smaller communities, learn to avoid the hysterical clamourings of gangs and groups. This was the sort of life he imagined – and had found – in Provence. In *The Great Trade Route* (1937), he wrote:

> I live in Provence, but I can't become a Provençal because that, as things go, would be to become French, and I don't want to become French for reasons that would take too long to tell . . . No, I want to belong to a nation of Small Producers, with some local, but no national feeling at all. Without boundaries, or armed forces, or customs, or government. That would never want me to kill anyone out of a group feeling. Something like being a Provençal. I might want to insult someone from the Gard if he said he could grow better marrows than we in the Var. But that would be as far as even local feeling would go.

The old advice about cultivating one's garden was always moral as well as practical; nor was it a counsel of quietism. As human beings recklessly use up the world's resources and despoil the planet, as the follies of globalisation become more apparent, as we head towards what could be the biggest smash of all, the wisdom and the way of living that Ford Madox Ford – literature's good soldier – found in Provence are perhaps even more worth attending to.

FORD'S ANGLICAN SAINT

I N 1927, FORD Madox Ford compared himself to a great
auk, that clumsy North Atlantic penguin, hunted to death
by the middle of the nineteenth century. The occasion was
the reissue of his first masterpiece *The Good Soldier* (1915) –
his 'great auk's egg' – which he had published at the age of
forty-one. Even back then, he maintained, he had felt like an
'extinct volcano', one who had had his time and was all too
willing to hand over to the 'clamorous young writers' of the
rising generation. But those new voices – Imagists, Vorticists,
Cubists – had been blown away by the Great War, and somehow
he was still around. And so, to his own surprise, 'I have come
out of my hole again' to write more books . . . Such weary,
genteel valetudinarianism was typical of Ford. When he died,
Graham Greene wrote that it felt like 'the obscure death of
a veteran – an impossibly Napoleonic veteran, say, whose
immense memory spanned the period from Jena to Sedan'.

However, it was and is always a mistake to go along with
Ford's self-presentation. He appeared confused and was often
confusing; he would say one thing and probably mean another,
only to state its opposite as a counter-certainty not very long
afterwards; he was fanciful, unreliable and exasperating. Some
thought him simply a liar, though as Ezra Pound charitably
pointed out to Hemingway, Ford 'only lied when he was very
tired'. So in 1927, for all his self-dismissingness, he was three-
quarters of the way through what would become his second
masterpiece: the four-book *Parade's End* (1924–8). A novel
which couldn't be further from the work of some

superannuated old buffer: in literary technique and human psychology, it is as modern and modernist as they come. And now that the years have shaken down, it is Ford who makes Greene look old-fashioned, rather than the other way round.

The Good Soldier's protagonist, Edward Ashburnham, was a version of the chivalric knight. *Parade's End*'s protagonist, Christopher Tietjens, is a version of the Anglican saint. Both are great auks making do in a world of modernity and muddle. Tietjens – a North Yorkshireman whose ancestors came over with 'Dutch William' – believes that the seventeenth century was 'the only satisfactory age in England'. He is 'a Tory of an extinct type' who has 'no politics that did not disappear in the eighteenth century'. He reads no poetry except Byron, thinks Gilbert White of Selborne 'the last English writer who could write', and approves of only one novel written since the eighteenth century (not that we can read it, since it is by a character in *Parade's End*). Both Ashburnham and Tietjens share a streak of romantic feudalism – nostalgia for a time of rights and duties and supposed orderliness. But Ashburnham is better fitted for the modern world, being – beneath his chivalric coating – a devious libertine and not outstandingly bright. Tietjens, by contrast, declares, 'I stand for monogamy and chastity. And for no talking about it.' He is also highly intelligent, with an encyclopedic memory – 'the most brilliant man in England', as we are frequently assured in the opening book, *Some Do Not*. This may be an advantage in the Imperial Department of Statistics, where he number-crunches for England; but isn't such a good idea in the world he inhabits.

There, intelligence is viewed as suspect and chastity weird; virtue as smugness, and saintliness a direct provocation. It is a great audacity for a novelist to begin a long novel with a main character whom very few other characters like, let alone admire. Tietjens is socially awkward, and emotionally reticent to the point of muteness: when, in the book's opening action, his wife Sylvia, having left him four months previously, asks to be taken back, he 'seemed to have no feelings about the matter'. He is 'completely without emotions that he could realise', and 'had not spoken more than twenty words about the event'. Later, he is said to have a 'terrifying expressionlessness'. Men sponge off him for both ideas and money; women on the whole find him rebarbative – 'his looks and his silences alarmed them'. In the course of the novel he is variously compared to a maddened horse, an ox, a swollen animal, a mad bullock, a lonely buffalo, a town bull, a raging stallion, a dying bulldog, a grey bear, a farmyard boar, a hog, and finally a dejected bulldog. He is also likened to a navvy, a sweep, a stiff Dutch doll and an immense feather mattress. He is 'lumpish, clumsy', with 'immense hands'. His wife constantly imagines him constructed from meal-sacks. Even Valentine Wannop, the spiky suffragette who is eventually to bring this Anglican saint a kind of salvation, initially finds him 'as mad as he is odious', with hateful eyes 'protruding at her like a lobster's'; she takes him for just another 'fat golfing idiot'. Still, for all his apparent ineptness, there is one thing always to be said for Christopher Tietjens: he is very good with horses.

Tietjens's notions of love and sex – which you would not expect to be conventional – are summed up at one point as follows: 'You seduced a young woman in order to be able to finish your talks to her.' Which is the exact opposite of one conventional male view, in which 'chatting up' with luck leads to sex, and afterwards you wonder what to talk about. (Tietjens's idea is a less engaging version of what Ford himself believed. As he put it, rather more sweetly, *in propria persona*: 'You marry to continue the conversation.') In Tietjens's mind, it is 'intimate conversation' which leads to 'the final communion of your souls . . . that in effect was love'. The sort of woman such an Anglican saint requires should be 'passionate yet circumspect'. The second adjective is richly inappropriate for Sylvia, who first seduced him, very uncircumspectly, in a railway carriage.

For Graham Greene, Sylvia Tietjens is 'surely the most possessed evil character in the modern novel'. A wife who is bored, promiscuous and up-to-date, tied to a husband who is omniscient, chaste and antique: there's a marriage made in hell. Christopher is a mixture of chivalry and masochism (if it hurts, I must be doing the right thing); Sylvia a mixture of recklessness and sadism (if it hurts him, I must be doing the right thing). Christopher believes that a gentleman does not divorce his wife, however she behaves; though if she wants to divorce him, he accepts it. He also thinks of Sylvia as a 'tremendous discipline' for the soul – rather as being in the French Foreign Legion would be for the body. Sylvia for her part cannot divorce Christopher because she is a Catholic. And so the couple are bound together on a wheel of fire. And the torments she devises for her husband are of exquisite accuracy. When she was thirteen (we learn only towards the end of the fourth volume, *Last Post*) Sylvia idly imagined cramming a kitten's paws into walnut shells; this shows great early skill of a sadic nature. Throughout the novel, she deploys the subtle rumour, the lie direct, and the vicious deed to visit on her husband a series of social, financial and psychological humiliations. Her final act of malignity is the cutting-down of the Great Tree of Groby at Tietjens's ancestral home – 'as nasty a blow as the Tietjens had had in generations'. Once, she had watched a fish eagle circling high above a scream of herring gulls, causing havoc by its mere presence; she liked and remembered this as a self-image. Still, for all her apparent viciousness, there is one thing always to be said for Sylvia Tietjens: she is very good with horses.

Why, you may ask, does she persecute her husband? Or, more particularly, why continue, year after year, when she has many admirers, from young bucks to old generals, fawning on her, seeking both her love and her body? Part of the answer lies in Christopher's very saintliness: the more he fails to respond and suffers without complaint, the more it goads her.

He also infuriatingly attempts to see things from her point of view. What could be more enraging to a soul like Sylvia's than to be understood and forgiven? And so, every time, she returns to the attack on her great meal-sack of a husband. She loathes him – for his gentlemanliness and solemnity, his passiveness, his 'pompous self-sufficiency', his 'brilliance' and the 'immorality' of the views which that brilliant mind emits. When her confessor, Father Consett, suggests that '*Tout savoir, c'est tout pardonner*' she replies that 'to know everything about a person is to be bored ... bored ... bored!' Sylvia is bored by marriage, but even more bored by promiscuity. 'All men are repulsive,' she assures her mother. And, 'man-mad' though she appears, Sylvia treats her lovers with disdain: they are not even worth properly tormenting. 'Taking up with a man', she reflects, 'was like reading a book you had read when you had forgotten that you had read it. You had not been for ten minutes in any sort of intimacy with a man before you said: "But I've read all this before."'

And this too, in a way, is her husband's fault. Their relationship is not just about the infliction and the bearing of pain. Key to an understanding of Sylvia are those rare moments when Ford, a profound psychologist, allows us to consider that Sylvia is more than just a vengeful spirit possessed by evil. However infuriating Tietjens might be, however 'immoral' his views, he is the only truly mature man she has been with, the only one whose conversation can hold her: 'As beside him, other men simply did not seem ever to have grown up.' So he has spoiled her for all other men, and must be punished for it. The more so because he is the only one who can still move her. In the middle of France, in the middle of war, when a venomous old French duchess seems about to derail a wedding, Tietjens, applying intelligence, practicality and his 'atrocious' old-fashioned French, talks the woman down. Sylvia has been watching, and: 'It almost broke Sylvia's heart to see how exactly Christopher did the right thing.' Two and a half novels later, when Tietjens is living with Valentine Wannop and Sylvia has almost reached the bottom of her bag of torments, she imagines confronting her husband's mistress: 'But he might come in, mooning in, and suddenly stiffen into a great, clumsy – oh, adorable – face of stone.' That 'oh, adorable' says it all. As far as Sylvia can love, she loves Tietjens; and her rage at him is a function of sexual passion. She still desires him, still wants to 'torment and allure' him; but one of the Anglican saint's conditions for her return to the marriage is that he will not sleep with her – a torment in riposte.

As all this suggests, the emotional level of the novel is high, and often close to hysteria. There is scarcely a character in the book – except, perhaps, Marie-Léonie, the Frenchly practical mistress of Christopher's brother Mark – who is not described at one time or another as being mad, or on the verge of madness. Only one – Captain McKechnie – seems positively certifiable, but for most, 'normality' means a kind of nerve-strained semi-madness. We might expect, for instance, that Valentine Wannop, the emotional counterweight to Sylvia, the virgin to her adulteress, who shares much with Tietjens – they are both Latinists with 'bread-and-butter brains', both 'without much of the romantic' to them, both lovers of frugality – that she at least would have a healthy mind in her undoubtedly healthy body. But even she finds her nerves constantly on edge and her mind slipping: her head 'seems to contain two balls of strings being separately unwound'. At one point, she barks an order to her own panicky thoughts: 'Steady the Buffs!' The mind at work is like a regiment under fire, and about to relocate; but where is it going, and who is leading it, and will it survive?

The middle two volumes of the novel are spent at the Western Front. Other, more conventional novelists might have set the madness of war against the calm and balm of love and sex;

Ford knows more and sees deeper. War and sexual passion are not opposites: they are in the same business, two parts of the same pincer attack on the sanity of the individual. It is not at first obvious the extent to which *Parade's End* is saturated with sex – with memories of it, hopes for it and rumours about it. (The novel is masterly on the workings of gossip, and the way it gets poisonously out of hand. By the fourth volume, the rumours about the Tietjens brothers have grown to the point where the pair of them are viewed as 'notorious libertines' and Mark said to be dying of syphilis. The objective reader can count the number of women the brothers appear to have slept with in their entire lives: three between the two of them.) The central emotional and sexual vortex is that involving Sylvia, Christopher and Valentine. But the lives of lesser characters, even those who are specks at the periphery of the reader's vision, are also endlessly disrupted and twisted by sex. There is O Nine Morgan, who applies for home leave because his wife is having an affair with a prizefighter; Tietjens, having heard that the boxer will kill Morgan if he turns up in Wales, refuses the request. So, instead of being beaten to death, O Nine is blown to bits in the trenches: sex gets him either way. Elsewhere, sergeants' wives take up with Belgians; a cook ruins his career by going AWOL because of his 'sister'; an RSM wants a commission because the 'bad boys' who 'monkey' with his wild daughter back home will be more careful if she's an officer's daughter; while Captain McKechnie keeps getting home leave to divorce, and then not divorcing ('That's modernism,' growls General Campion). Sylvia's brusque view of the military is that 'You went to war when you desired to rape innumerable women.' She regards the war as an *agapemone* (a place where free love is practised), and as 'an immense warlock's carnival of appetites, lusts, ebrieties'.

But no one in the novel gets sex, and sexual passion, right. Sex is almost always damaging and disastrous – to the extent that the businesslike relationship between Mark and

Marie-Léonie seems almost normal, until you consider that
in the thirteen years she has been his mistress she has never
known 'what his Office was nor where his chambers, nor even
his surname'. Towards the very end of the novel there is a
walk-on (or rather, ride-on) part for Christopher and Sylvia's
son. He is just a downy boy, if one beginning to feel the allure
of an older woman; but he is old enough to have witnessed
his mother at work on various men. And what is this ingenu's
early conclusion on the whole matter? 'But wasn't sex a terrible
thing.' Nor does the instinct just do for human beings. Christopher, on a balmy day in the Seine valley, the war for once
distant, hears a skylark singing so far out of season that he
concludes 'the bird must be over-sexed'. Two novels later, his
brother Mark, lying awake, hears nightingales producing not
their normal, beautiful sound, but something much coarser,
which seems to him to contain abuse of other males, and
boastfulness to their own sitting hens. It is the sound, in his
phrase, of 'sex ferocity'.

   Greene wrote that '*The Good Soldier* and the Tietjens series
seem to me almost the only adult novels dealing with the
sexual life that have been written in English. They are our
answer to Flaubert.' In subject matter, certainly; but there is
also a consanguinity in technique. One of Flaubert's great
developments (not inventions – no one really invents anything
in the novel) was *style indirect libre*, that way of dipping into
a character's consciousness – for a paragraph, a sentence, a few
words, sometimes for just a single word – showing things from
his or her point of view, and then dipping out again. This is
a direct ancestor of the stream-of-consciousness narrative so
richly deployed by Ford. Much of *Parade's End* takes place
within the heads of its characters: in memory and anticipation,
reflection, misunderstanding and self-justification. Few novelists
have better understood and conveyed the overworkings of the
hysterical brain, the underworkings of the damaged brain (after
his first spell at the front, Tietjens returns with partial memory

loss), the slippings and slidings of the mind at the end of its
tether, with all its breakings-in and breakings-off.

The name Freud occurs only once, on Sylvia's lips: 'I . . .
pin my faith on Mrs Vanderdecken [a society role model].
And, of course, Freud.' She doesn't elucidate, though we might
reasonably deduce that he provides her with some theoretical
justification for what Tietjens calls 'her high-handed divaga-
tions from fidelity'. But Freud is more widely present, if – since
this is a very English novel – in a subtle, anglicised form: 'In
every man there are two minds that work side by side, the
one checking the other.' The word 'subconscious' is never used;
instead, Tietjens at one point has been 'thinking with his
undermind'. Later, Valentine had always known something
'under her mind'; Tietjens refers to 'something behind his
mind'; while General Campion 'was for the moment in high
good humour on the surface, though his subordinate minds
[sic] were puzzled and depressed'. Ford moves between these
levels of the mind as he moves between fact and memory,
certainty and impression. Tietjens compares the mind to a
semi-obedient dog. Nor is it just mind, memory and fact that
are slipping and sliding; it is the very language used to describe
them. General Campion, one of the least hysterical of characters, is driven to wonder, 'What the *hell* is language for? We
go round and round.'

The narrative also goes round and round, backtracking
and criss-crossing. A fact, or an opinion, or a memory will be
dropped in, and often not explained for a dozen or a hundred
pages. Sometimes this may be a traditional cliffhanger: a character left in a state of emotional crisis while the novel ducks
off for fifty or sixty pages at the Western Front. More often,
the device becomes something much more individual and
Fordian. An explosive piece of information, murderous lie or
raging emotional conclusion might casually be let drop, whereupon the narrative will back off, as if shocked by anything
stated with such certainty, then circle around, come close again,

back off again and, finally, approach it directly. The narrative, in other words, is acting as the mind often works. This can confuse, but as V. S. Pritchett said of Ford, 'Confusion was the mainspring of his art as a novelist. He confused to make clear.' To say that a great novel needs reading with great attention is somewhere between a banality and an insult. But it applies particularly to *Parade's End*. It will be a very rare reader who does not intermittently look up from the page to ask, 'But did I know that? Have we been told that already or not?' In what sense did Christopher 'kill' his father? Did we know that Mrs Macmaster was even pregnant, let alone that she had lost a child? Have we been told Tietjens is under arrest? That his stepmother died of grief when Sylvia left him? That Macmaster was dead? Has Mark really been struck dumb? And so on, confusingly and clarifyingly, to the very end.

Since nothing is simple with Ford, one of the unsimple things about *Parade's End* is the status and quality of the fourth volume, *Last Post*. When putting together the Bodley Head edition of Ford (1962–3), Greene simply omitted it, thus reducing a quartet to a trilogy. He thought the book 'was more than a mistake – it was a disaster, a disaster which has delayed a full critical appreciation of *Parade's End*'. He charged it with sentimentality, and with damagingly clearing up 'valuable ambiguities' by bringing them into 'the idyllic sunshine of Christopher's successful escape into the life of a Kentish small-holder'.

Half a century on, it's hard to see *Last Post* as having delayed 'a full critical appreciation' of *Parade's End*. Cyril Connolly, in *The Modern Movement* (1965), followed Greene by referring to Ford's 'war trilogy' (and patronisingly dismissed all of it), but most subsequent editors have chosen to view it as a quartet rather than a trilogy. And over those years, the reputations of both Ford and the novel itself have remained

pretty much what they always have been. Ford enthusiasts are
ever in the minority and ever undeterred. To be a Fordite is
rather like being a member of one of those volunteer groups
who help restore Britain's canal system. You run into them,
muddy and sweaty, spending their Sunday afternoons digging
out some long-disused arm which once brought important
goods to and from, say, Wendover. You are fairly sure that they
are doing a good thing, but unless you jump down and get
muddy yourself, the virtue of the task, indeed of the whole
canal system, might well escape you.

There is a clear structural argument in favour of *Last Post*:
the first volume of the quartet is set before the war and the
middle two during it; so a fourth, post-war volume makes
sense. But it's also true that if, when you got to the end of
the third volume, *A Man Could Stand Up*, you were told that
this was the last Ford ever had to say about Tietjens, you
would not necessarily be shocked or disappointed. That novel
ends in the chaos of Armistice Night 1918, with a proper
melee of the drunk and the half-mad, of celebration and high
anxiety, of possible new beginnings, and of Tietjens and Valentine at last together, dancing. Six pages before the end of the
third volume, she has smiled at him for the first time. And
the novel's final line, from inside Valentine's head, is a typical
and brilliant Fordian aposiopesis: 'She was setting out on . . .'

It could end there. We could imagine to ourselves what
she (and Tietjens) were setting out on – and it would, no
doubt, be that life they separately and together dreamed of, a
life of talking, talking, of continuing the conversation; also of
an escape from the past, and war, and madness, and Sylvia.
That is probably what we would write for the two of them.
What Ford in fact wrote is different, and more complicated,
and darker, and really not very much as Greene describes it
– 'the idyllic sunshine of Christopher's successful escape into
the life of a Kentish small-holder'. In fact, it's West Sussex, not
Kent, and Christopher is a furniture dealer rather than a

smallholder; but let that pass. 'Idyllic', 'successful'? Well, Christopher the saint is still being cheated by the world's wicked, while he and Valentine (plus Christopher's mute, paralysed brother Mark and his mistress, now wife, Marie-Léonie) get by financially thanks to occasional windfalls and some effective French housekeeping. Valentine has patched clothes and collapsing underwear, and for all their shared ambition of frugality she finds it hard going. Anxieties are not reduced (Valentine, having secured Tietjens, is now constantly worried about losing him); a sense of madness is never far away; and hovering over their supposedly idyllic escape is the fish eagle Sylvia, thinking up further attacks on not just her estranged husband but also his pregnant girlfriend and paralysed brother.

Ford structures this grim continuation with characteristic boldness. The first half is mediated through the non-speaking Mark, who recapitulates and reorders and re-examines the past; then we are much with Sylvia as she plans fresh revenges and her own social advancement; also with Marie-Léonie as she bottles cider; then, a little towards the end, with Valentine. And so, through this final volume, there mounts the increasing question: where is Christopher Tietjens? He is often referred to, but his presence and point of view are conspicuously and risingly absent until the last two pages when he returns, worn out, from a failed attempt to save the Great Tree of Groby (no 'success' there). Where is this idyll with Valentine? It exists only in the siting of the house, with a view of four counties, in its neat horticulture, its woods and hedges. The surroundings may be idyllic, but any romance lies strictly in nature not humankind. Where is that talking, that continued conversation? Not in *Last Post* – nor is there any back-reference to its having already occurred. Sylvia may furiously envy the household for having found 'peace', but the reader witnesses little of this; it may all be in Sylvia's fantasy.

Consider the only scene which shows Tietjens and Valentine together, in those final two pages. He returns from Yorkshire carrying 'a lump of wood' (it is 'aromatic', so presumably a chunk of the Great Tree). Valentine's greeting consists of a rebuke for his incompetence as an antiques dealer: he has foolishly left some prints in a jar which has now been taken away by someone else. 'How could you? How could you? How are we going to feed and clothe a child if you do such things?' She tells him to go off and get the prints back at once. Mark (now speaking again) points out to her that 'the poor devil's worn out'. But this appeal has no effect. Then: 'Heavily, like a dejected bulldog, Christopher made for the gate. As he went up the green path beyond the hedge, Valentine began to sob. "How are we to live? How are we ever to live?"'

Is this an idyllic escape? There is more than a hint that Tietjens's inept saintliness is bringing out the scold in Valentine. The fish-eagle silhouette of Sylvia may have finally fled the sky (though she has changed her mind so often before that who is to say her private armistice will last?); but Ford allows us to imagine that, just as the anxious will always find new anxieties to replace the old, so a tormented saint, freed from his persecutor, might yet bring upon himself a new tormentor in the unlikeliest of shapes. Anglican saints were always hunted to extinction, just like great auks.

KIPLING'S FRANCE

IN 1878, LOCKWOOD Kipling, principal of the Mayo
College of Art in Lahore, took his twelve-year-old son to
the Paris exhibition. Lockwood was involved with the
Indian section of arts and manufactures; he gave the young
Rudyard two francs a day for food, a free pass to the exhibition, and left him to his own devices. The boy, who all his
life was to love seeing how things were put together, was
enthralled by 'all the wonders of all the worlds emerging from
their packing cases'.

One of his favourite sights was the head of Bartholdi's
Statue of Liberty, soon to be shipped to New York as a belated
centennial gift to the American republic. For five centimes
– or a free pass – you could climb an internal staircase and
look out at the world through the vacant eyeballs. Rudyard
frequently made the ascent, and on one occasion an elderly
French wiseacre advised him, 'Now, young Englisher, you can
say that you have looked through the eyes of Liberty herself.'
Fifty-five years later, the elderly Kipling remembered this
conveniently placed oracle, and chose to correct him: 'He
spoke less than the truth. It was through the eyes of France
that I began to see.'

Kipling and France? Kipling and India obviously. Kipling
and England, Kipling and the Empire, Kipling and South
Africa, Kipling and the United States, Kipling and the hated
Germany (the true home, in Orwell's analysis, to those often
mislocated 'lesser breeds without the law'). But Kipling and
France? It's not an obvious runner. France and the French

feature little in his published work. Nor might you expect this demotic, pragmatic, self-educated celebrant of the British Empire to care much for the lofty and theoretical inhabitants of Britain's closest imperial rival. Yet that first visit of 1878 began something which continued until Kipling's death in 1936. As his daughter Elsie noted simply after her father's death, 'He was always happy in France.'

Happy in, certainly; happy with, not always. In later life Kipling was inclined to make his relationship with the country seem like one of seamless felicity. But in the 1880s and 90s, when imperial rivalries were at their sharpest, Kipling was reliably anti-French; from India, he wrote journalistic defences of Britain in 'what I then conceived to be parodies of Victor Hugo's more extravagant prose'. The Boer War – in which the French were noticeably not on the British side – made things worse. Kipling wrote a mocking story, 'The Bonds of Discipline', in which the crew of a British cruiser outwit a stowaway French spy.

This passage of geopolitical froideur ended with the *Entente Cordiale* in 1904. After this there were no grounds for scowling at France. There was also now a means by which the novelist could renew his passion and deepen his knowledge of the country: the motor car. Like Edith Wharton, Conrad and Ford Madox Ford, Kipling was entranced by the new century's first great invention. In the autumn of 1899 he had hired an appropriately named Embryo; the following summer he bought a steam-driven American Locomobile; next came a Lanchester, personally delivered to the famous author by Mr Lanchester himself.

In March 1910 Kipling was staying at Vernet-les-Bains, the Pyrenean spa where his wife Carrie annually took the sulphur baths. Claude Johnson, joint manager of Rolls & Co, and also first secretary of the Royal Automobile Club, cannily made Kipling an offer he could scarcely refuse: 'I am sending my car back to Paris empty. If you would care to take her over, she is at your disposition.' Since the car had 'all the power of the Horses of the Sun' and came with a chauffeur who had been a Royal Marine and knew the world 'largely and particularly', Kipling was delighted. The Silver Phantom took them from Banyuls-sur-Mer, 'where we gathered narcissi in a field and wisteria was in bloom', via Perpignan, Narbonne, Montpellier, Nîmes, Arles, Avignon, Tournon, St-Étienne, Moulins, Nevers and Montargis to Fontainebleau and Paris. It was on this trip that Kipling first became fascinated with the dead city of Les Baux – 'a vast stone Golgotha, inconceivably mad and grotesque and pathetic'; he discovered the roads of France – 'straight, wide, level, perfect', a judgement later needing qualification; and he was hooked on the Rolls-Royce. The following year he bought his own and never subsequently changed marque. (At Bateman's, his house in Sussex, you can inspect his last, shimmeringly dark blue Roller.) He also began the habit of annual motor tours of France, which continued – with the interruption of the Great War – until the late 1920s.

In 2000, the publishing director of Macmillan was clearing out his desk after forty years with the firm. The desk had previously belonged to Thomas Mark, Kipling's editor. In its furthest recesses were six small leather-bound notebooks. These turned out to be the motor-tour diaries Kipling kept from 1911 to 1926 – the only diaries of his to have survived apart from an extract from an Indian journal of 1884. They have yet to be published; but the transcripts – running to nearly a hundred pages – vividly convey the mentality and the obsessiveness of this writer-as-traveller.

For some of those early literary motorists, like Edith Wharton, the car was largely a means to an end: the end being distant people and far-flung cultural monuments. She savoured the exhilaration of motor travel but ignored its specifics and technicalities; the car was a clever mechanical servant, and if it got uppity, her husband Teddy and the chauffeur were there to deal with it. Kipling, who was whizzing around France at the same time, found the means as absorbing as the end.

Like other well-heeled tourists, he naturally visited the key sites – Carcassonne, Chartres, the church at Brou, the Bayeux Tapestry, Albi Cathedral, Fontaine-de-Vaucluse. He loved clambering around things, whether Chartres Cathedral to examine the back of a stained-glass window, or a Dordogne cave to see 'Cro-Magnon piccys of bison, horse, wolf and rhino'. But Kipling was the most democratic of English geniuses, equally at ease with generals and peasants, as interested by inner tubes as by high art. He travels as the great man in his Rolls-Royce, as the speech-writer of George V and friend of Clemenceau (who visited Bateman's more than once); but he also travels as Pooterish motor-nerd. He loved totting up the distances covered; he noted each puncture suffered by his Rolls – 'a terror on tyres' – and tried every possible brand of tyre, even to Russian Provodniks. 'New Goodyear tyre,' he notes, 'car pulled like silk.' 'English springs aren't strong enough for French roads – that's a fact.' 'T had adjusted carburettor and she pulled like a dragon.' 'The succeeding days were devoted to the care of the Duchess and . . . not only was her spring renewed but all her transmission noise was eliminated by Parsons.' 'A most annoying day as far as tyres went but this scenery and climate beyond words' – this from one rarely beyond words.

One of Kipling's least-known literary modes was as writer of reports on both roads and accommodation for the AA and the RAC. In 1911, after his first tour in his own vehicle, he filled up the RAC's confidential touring report form. 'Hôtel Metropole, Montpellier. Bad, dear and greedy. They try the old trick of charging extra franc on wine ordered from wine list in restaurant hoping guest will not notice on paying bill. Should be spoken to severely.' 'Angoulême – Hôtel de France. Lunch only – very good food and sanitary arrangements clean.'

'Bergerac – De Londres et des Voyageurs. Not over clean; food only fair, reasonable charges and obliging. Sanitary arrangements old-fashioned and dirty, impossible for ladies until cleaned. No baths.' Kipling inspecting French hotels is like an RSM faced with a particularly shabby intake of recruits. Even if your overall turnout is satisfactory, Old Kipper will always spot that tiny smudge on your gaiter. His report on the Hôtel Bernard in Carcassonne ends: 'Note. Letter-box in hall unsatisfactory being small and casual.'

This RAC inspector of toilets and letter boxes, we shouldn't forget, had been awarded the Nobel Prize for Literature only four years previously. But this didn't temper his relentless and quotidian curiosity. 24 March 1914: 'Grand Hôtel de Grenoble is not too good, and they also charged 5fr to wash car which I must report to AA.' Five days later, in Chartres: 'As usual, bathroom *Hot* was cold. Had some talk with a man in a 1905 Wolseley.' 4 May 1921: 'arr. Newhaven 4.25, but not away (in heavy shower) til 5.20. All quite smooth but slow. Must write AA.' Despite the chauffeur-driven Rolls, despite the fact that he walked with captains and kings, the Kipling who emerges from these notes is an archetypal motorist, occasionally joyful but mostly fretful and frustrated. 'Cabourg to Caen: road crowded. 76 cars in 31 miles!' 'Lost way between Dreux and Nonancourt – never trust nice strangers.' 'First time I used Michelin map which I found very convenient.' 'Lunched in wet pines by roadside with a tin of unopenable foie gras.'

Why did Kipling love France? Like many other Francophiles, he responded to its 'immense and amazing beauty'. He liked its food – preferably solid rather than grand, and at a reasonable price. 'They understand belly-service in Alsace,' he noted; while his daughter recalled 'a long detour in a day's motoring to sample the pigs' trotters in a town noted for this delicacy, and which a French general had said should not be missed'. In his poem 'France' (1913), he described the country as 'Furious in luxury, merciless in toil'. Kipling was not much interested in French luxury, and whereas others, having begun by admiring the landscape and the food, might continue gourmandising on the culture, the sense of style, the social or intellectual milieux and the *douceur de vivre*, he preferred to admire what many overlooked: the merciless toil.

It was a country that worked, and worked hard and efficiently. In India, Kipling had met forestry officials expertly trained by the French at Nancy. After the Great War he witnessed the extraordinary resilience and fortitude with which the French cleared up the wreckage and started again. On his motor tours he discovered pastoral and agricultural virtue, admiring villages and farmsteads where women, children and even dogs worked to full capacity. In 1933 he published *Souvenirs of France*, sixty pages (out of print ever since) of memory, praise, nostalgia and gratitude. There he recalls visiting an agricultural fair in the provinces and inspecting various appliances. 'I asked an agent how long a certain manure-pump would last – *marche* being the word I used. The answer was illuminating. "If you leave it lying out in winters, as you English do, it will not *marche* more than two years. Give it shelter and it will *marche* for 10."'

In a speech to the Royal Society of St George in 1922, Kipling claimed that for the English, the French were 'the only other people in the world that mattered' (probably untrue then, certainly now). In 'France' he calls the two countries 'Each the other's mystery, terror, need and love'. Perhaps what he most admired in France was what he thought his own country could do with more of. Work ethic, thrift, simplicity; 'the acceptance of hard living which fortifies the moral interior as small pebbles assist the digestion of fowls'. Self-discipline; but also external discipline. One aspect of social life that distinguished France and much of Continental Europe from Britain before the Great War was conscription. Kipling believed that a period of enforced military service promoted not only civic virtue but also a fundamental seriousness of mind which he felt his compatriots lacked. A Frenchman once said to him: 'How can you English understand our minds if you do not realise those years of service – those years of service for us all? When we come to talk to you about life it is like talking about death to children.'

If Kipling took France to his heart, the attachment became mutual. He seems to us such an English writer, such a British imperialist, such a pungent purveyor of the lore and language of his tribe, that it comes as a surprise to find how well known and widely read he was in France. On 26 March 1913 his motor-notes show him sheltering from the rain in Bourges Cathedral, 'where met highly intelligent young French priest who knew all about the *Jungle Book*. Gratifying to notice the spread of civilisation in Gaul.' General Nivelle gave him a tour of the front line in 1915, and with a gesture to the French troops under his command, remarked, 'All these men know your books.' Kipling smiled at the presumed civility, but Nivelle then took him to another sector where 'Sentries with rifles told me the same thing. Weird non-coms in dugouts echoed it till I nearly thought it was a put up job of the general. But 'twasn't. 'Twas true.'

Nor were his fans just among the poilus. 'I only dreamed of the jungle,' Jules Renard confided to his journal, 'Kipling has been there.' A few months before his death in 1893, the critic and philosopher Hippolyte Taine had *The Light That Failed* read to him by his nephew André Chevrillon. '*C'est un homme de génie*,' commented Taine; and Chevrillon attested that his uncle had never previously applied the G-word to any living writer. The novel – Kipling's only attempt at the longer form – was generally more admired in France than England. Sarah Bernhardt offered to produce a stage version; and Kipling concluded in his autobiography, 'I always fancied that it walked [*sic*] better in translation than in the original.'

One consequence of this French fame was that anonymity
on the motor tours was hard to preserve. Kipling's family used
to say that three days was the maximum they could stay in
one place without his identity being discovered. A soldier
would accost him in the street and bear him off to the nearest
officers' mess; a priest would make an occasion of his visit to
a church; by the third day, the mayor would be threatening a
civic reception and they would all have to flee.

Kipling's French, according to his biographer Charles
Carrington, 'was fluent, though inaccurate, and powerfully
helped out by gestures'. At school, he had been taught the
language with the help of a clever trick:

> I was 'invited' to study French. 'You'll never be able
> to talk it, but if I were you, I'd try to read it,' was [the
> master's] word. I append here the method of instruc-
> tion. Give an English boy the first half of *Twenty
> Thousand Leagues Under the Sea* in his native tongue.
> When he is properly intoxicated, withdraw it and
> present to him the second half in the original. After-
> wards – not before – Dumas the Prince of *amuseurs*,
> and the rest as God pleases.

Verne and Dumas led to Balzac, Rabelais and Maupassant;
he found Scarron 'dreary' and Anatole France 'a fraud'. He
also read Colette, whose animal stories he judged 'so much
better than mine'. In a letter of 1919 to André Chevrillon, he
mentions his early reading, adds a life of Dumas that made
his head 'spin with excitement and inchoate ideas', but
concludes: 'Otherwise the French influences (except a few
days in Paris in '78) seem to have been few.' Two years later,
receiving an honorary doctorate at the Sorbonne and doubtless playing a little to the occasion, he made the debt sound
greater: 'I will not confess (what must be evident to my literary
confrères here) how much in my art I have learned and applied

both consciously and unconsciously from the masters of that art in your country.'

The truth lies somewhere in between. Direct literary influence is small. Kipling called *The Light That Failed* 'a sort of inverted, metagrobolised phantasmagoria' on Prévost's *Manon Lescaut*. He also used French settings in three of his late stories – 'The Miracle of Saint Jubanas', 'The Bull That Thought' and 'Teem'; strangely, in the last two of these he used French animals (a Camargue bull and a Périgourdin truffle hound) as running metaphors for the artist and his travails. But overall, French influence on Kipling is of a more diffuse kind. Put Rabelais, Balzac and Maupassant together and – against the background of late-nineteenth-century English Literature – they make an argument against gentility and for specificity. Kipling was much accused of 'vulgarity' and 'cruelty' – in other words, of being democratic in personnel and truthful in theme and detail. An early exposure to French literature would have endorsed this aesthetic.

Angus Wilson was rather snooty about Kipling's Francophilia. 'Perhaps the love is a little self-conscious, a little the stereotype of France made by many Englishmen, especially of the upper-middle classes, in the 1920s, when many of them decided to settle there.' But Kipling's attachment to France was much more than that of a motor tourist who found the climate an improvement and the peasantry picturesque. It was a bond made lifelong – and sealed with blood – by the Great War. The sealing was both general and personal. Addressing a university banquet at Strasbourg in 1921, he expressed British losses with a comparison pitched directly for his audience. From Calais to Reims, he told them, 'We English have left there, a larger army than Napoleon left in Russia – 400,000 of the bodies of our own sons, beside a multitude of whom no trace remains.' He went on: 'They died with your sons. Have we forgotten where they died? Ask any man or woman

in any English street or field. They will give you at once the
name of some little demolished French village of which,
perhaps, even you have never heard. They will tell you the
very turn of road to it, the very hedge beside the orchard
where their man fell.'

Some of his audience would have known that among the
'multitude of whom no trace remains' was Kipling's only son,
John; and that the father could indeed give his last known
address – near Red House, on the edge of Chalk-Pit Wood,
among some slag heaps and miners' cottages. John Kipling
volunteered at the outbreak of war, a few days before his
seventeenth birthday; rather humiliatingly, he was refused on
grounds of poor sight. His (equally short-sighted) father used
his influence to wangle the boy a commission in the Irish
Guards; he was shipped out to France in August 1915, and by
the end of September was among the 20,000 British dead at
the Battle of Loos. Kipling's response was grief, pride, silence
and, after the war, ceaseless, detailed work for the War Graves
Commission. It was he who proposed the inscription on the
Stone of Sacrifice in the military cemeteries: 'Their name
liveth for evermore'. He drafted texts for memorials to the
British dead in French cathedrals; was responsible for the
nightly ceremony of the Last Post at the Menin Gate; and
was one of the originators of the plan to bury an Unknown
Soldier in Westminster Abbey.

What his motor-tour diaries reveal is that he was just as
assiduous an inspector of graveyards as ever he was of French
hotels. In one three-day period in 1924 he visited twenty-four
cemeteries. Now, shadowed by the death of his son, Kipling's
dry, methodical notes take on a terrible poignancy. 'Dury. No
headstones. Stones stacked for a year.' 'Ferme Buterne: bad
right of way – inaccessibility.' 'Cemetery register top and sides
need painting – book inside all damp and register inside will
go to pieces if not kept dry.' '4.50. St Mary's A. D. S. Spoilt
by gardener's shed.' 'Arras Road. (No book), a tiny (Canadian)

cemetery beautifully flowered, alone in a ploughed field, and the farmer pinching with his plough into the right of way. To report this.' 'NOTE. Nothing but the smallest plants should be set in front of the headstones as they hide the relatives' texts.'

On 13 May 1922, at Meerut: 'Cemetery austere and dignified – in spite of bake-house crematorium on corner where Hindus had been burned. All sorts burned here inside stone wall, spaced with what should be dignified evergreens (like cypresses) in years to come . . . Went round graves, spoke to gardeners, etc etc. I saw grave of Gunga Din, dooly-bearer.' Kipling worked as a War Graves Commissioner for the last eighteen years of his life, from 1918 to 1936. He gave intense support to this vast, unprecedented act of national remembering. Every fallen soldier was to be reburied in a marked grave, each with his own headstone; and there was a particular, unassuageable pain in the fact that Kipling could bow his head before the grave of Gunga Din and 400,000 others, but not before that of his son John, whose body was not identified until the 1990s.

As part of his work as a commissioner, Kipling visited the military cemetery in Rouen. 'Mar. 13 1925,' his motor-diary records, 'Got into Rouen (de la Poste) @ 10.30. Put small things into our rooms and went off at once to Cemetery (3,400 headstones up out of 11,000) where saw the gardener and contractor. All the place has been levelled and looks sloppy and dirty.' Of course, Kipling had by this time inspected scores of cemeteries and met numerous gardeners, and there is no sign from the rest of the day's notes that this was any different. He went to the marketplace in Rouen 'to do penance where Joan was burned' (he was a great devotee of the Maid and seriously apologetic over her immolation), then 'a bad dinner but decent champagne and so to bed'.

But the next day his motor diary makes unprecedented reference to work in progress. 'Have begun a few lines on the story of Helen Turrell and her "nephew" and the gardener in the great 20,000 cemetery.' On and off for the next ten days he records progress on 'The Gardener', one of his greatest short stories, a tale – like his own post-war life – of rigidly suppressed grief. As Kipling's quote marks suggest, Michael Turrell is not Helen's nephew but her illegitimate son, and her social shame compounds her suffering as she endures the cycle of pain Kipling had known ten years previously: from the 'inevitable series of unprofitable emotions' when Michael is posted missing, to the 'physical loathing of the living and returned young', whose presence emphasises her loss. Helen Turrell's epiphany comes at the Hagenzeele Third Cemetery in Belgium. Lost among the countless, counted dead, she asks a gardener where she can find her 'nephew', and with 'infinite compassion' he replies, Christlike, 'Come with me and I will show you where your son lies.' Since the story ends with this shimmer of the transcendental, it's worth noting that Kipling and his Roller passed through Lourdes the day before he finished it; although, typically, he observed to his diary that the town was 'quite empty and no miracles going on'.

In old age, despite having his cars 'put down', Kipling continued to visit France. He wintered in Monte Carlo and Cannes, while noting, as early as 1926, that 'the motor car has made the Riviera an hell – and a noisy, smelly one'. The last two decades of his life were lived with acute and recurrent abdominal pain, heroically resisted (once, in Paris, doubled up in agony, he clutched a cushion to himself and said, 'I think this time I'm going to have twins'). He constantly feared cancer; over a seventeen-year period nine different British doctors offered eight different diagnoses; in 1921 all his teeth were extracted, to no beneficial effect.

In 1933 he fell seriously ill in Paris, and a French doctor correctly deduced that he had been suffering from duodenal ulcers. It was by now too late to operate, and Kipling died

– in London, on his way to Cannes – three years later. But if it was 'through the eyes of France that I began to see', it was fitting that France also spoke to him one final, diagnostic truth.

FRANCE'S KIPLING

WHEN TALKING ABOUT my novel *Arthur & George*
I am sometimes asked – by a deerstalkered profile
in the shadows of the bookshop – how my fascination with Sir Arthur Conan Doyle began. My answer often
comes as a disappointment: I was drawn to the story, I explain,
by its other eponym, George. Arthur came inevitably attached
to him. I would have been just as happy – indeed perhaps
happier – if my novelist-as-man-of-action had been someone
else: Kipling, for instance. I choose the name deliberately,
because the two writers were virtual coevals; further, they
were friends, fellow imperialists, men of loud public opinions,
and golf companions who once played a round together in
the snows of Vermont with the balls painted red.

While a slight air of let-down may be sensed in my ques-
tioner, I also find – as is often the case when answering
questions in public – a contradicting surtitle running through
my head. Would I have been just as happy? Happier? True,
Kipling was by far the greater writer, recognised as a genius
even by those (such as Henry James and Max Beerbohm)
who were at the distant end of the aesthetic spectrum; but
would this make him an easier, or more fulfilling, subject than
a fine professional storyteller who happened to have created
a literary archetype? What if Kipling had come attached to
my story and I had found him impossible to recreate imagina-
tively? He was prickly and private (though this could have
been an advantage); he regarded any form of biographical
venture as the 'Higher Cannibalism'; he even left us a famous

admonitory 'Appeal' – 'And for the little, little span / The
dead are borne in mind / Seek not to question other than /
The books I left behind.' Was it, in fact, possible to put Kipling
into a novel at all?

Jérôme and Jean Tharaud clearly thought so: their roman
à clef, *Dingley, l'illustre écrivain*, was first published in 1902
under the editorial direction of Charles Péguy, then rewritten
and republished in 1906. It was a popular success, won the
Prix Goncourt, and was translated within the year into Spanish
and German – though never into English. Kipling's biographer
Charles Carrington stoutly dismissed it as 'plainly a hostile
criticism of Rudyard Kipling presented in the form of a
romance', but others detected more literary virtue. André Gide
wrote in his Journal for 9 January 1907: 'I greatly admire the
work of the Tharaud brothers on their *Dingley*, of which I
am reading the excellent revision. But how this sort of
reworking several years after the event amazes me and remains
foreign to me!' Gide's praise is, admittedly, offered in the
context of greater self-praise ('I cannot, I have never been
able to, rewrite a sentence later; all the work that I put on it
must be when it is still in a molten state; and each sentence
strikes me as perfect only when retouching has become impossible'), but even so. Gide rarely read anything that was less
than serious.

The Tharauds were born at Saint-Junien in the Haute-
Vienne (Jérôme in 1874, Jean three years later) and brought
up in Angoulême, then Paris. Jérôme was a fellow student of
Péguy at the École Normale Supérieure; Jean became secretary
to the novelist and mystico–nationalist Maurice Barrès. The
brothers – no doubt following the example of the Goncourts
– first set up as co-authors in 1898 with a novel called *Le
Coltineur débile*, and continued their creative association for
the next half-century. The younger would write the first draft,
then the elder would correct, adjust and fine-tune. Exoticists
after the fashion of Pierre Loti (they wrote of Palestine, Persia,

Romania, and were in Morocco at the same time as Edith Wharton), they were also 'shrewd and solid Limousins', as my 1920s literary *Larousse* informs me. 'They are by nature optimists and the pity they feel in the presence of misfortune springs less from their suffering hearts than from their capacity to understand everything. They have the melancholy of the widely read who in all circumstances remain clear-sighted witnesses.' Yes, the French always have written about literature in a different way.

The Tharauds began writing at a time when the French and British empires were at a high point of rivalry, and French responses to Kipling were a microcosm of broader geopolitical attitudes. Like their most famous novelist, the British were more active, more vulgar, more can-do. Their empire was bigger and brasher than that of the French; and the Fashoda Incident had recently brought the two powers to the edge of intercolonial war. To the British, Fashoda was and remains just a strange place name at or beyond the margins of memory; to the French, an event hugely magnified by propaganda and lost pride. In July 1898, eight French and 120 Senegalese soldiers arrived at a ruined fort on the Sudanese Upper Nile, having spent two years crossing the continent to get there (Frenchly, they set off equipped with 1,300 litres of claret, 50 bottles of Pernod and a mechanical piano). They raised the *tricolore* and planted a garden. Their main purpose was to annoy the British, and they did, a little: Kitchener turned up with a sizeable force and advised them to leave. He also gave them copies of French newspapers, in which they read of the Dreyfus case and wept. The two sides fraternised, the matter was handed over to the politicians, and six months later a British band played the Marseillaise as the French withdrew. No one was hurt, let alone killed. How could this not have been just a tiny comic sideshow? But that is a British response (also, one from the side that forced the withdrawal). To the French, it was a key moment of national humiliation and dishonour. It also made a profound impact on a certain six-year-old French boy, who in later years remembered it as 'a childhood tragedy'. How was Kitchener to know, as he was drinking warm champagne with eight Frenchmen at that distant fort, that this encounter would play out, four decades later, in de Gaulle's obstreperous, anglophobe behaviour in wartime London exile, and six decades later in his triple refusal to allow Britain to join the Common Market?

Though the name Dingley has only a chiming resemblance to Kipling, any pretence of artistic or legal disguise vanishes from the opening lines of the Tharauds' novel: 'Everywhere that English was spoken, the name of Dingley, the famous writer, was known. Even children were familiar with it: they learned to read from his books. In truth, he was a man with an incomparable freshness of imagination. He seemed to have been born at the very dawn of the world, at a time when the senses of our distant ancestors were still as keen as those of the beasts.' This Dingley has quartered the globe in both his life and his work, combining within himself 'the active instincts of the English race with the dreaminess and questing soul of the Hindu'; he has 'become familiar with glory at an age when a man is still able to enjoy it'; and he has written a tale which translates back into English as 'The Finest Story in the World'. He is now in his forties, 'a small man with dry, angular features, the upper lip defended by a bristly moustache, and grey eyes lying in wait behind steel-rimmed spectacles'.

So: Kipling, with one or two minor variations or ignorances (like giving the writer an Oxford education). But as the reference to his incomparable imagination suggests, this is a subtler portrait than Carrington implies. Dingley's genius, his energy, his ceaseless curiosity are all acknowledged; what is questioned is the use to which the famous imagination and the public fame are put. There is also the charge − equally made against Kipling in England − that the writer's aesthetic has become compromised by his temperament. Perhaps the novel's key line is: 'His passion for the picturesque had stifled his sense of human sympathy.' A parallel complaint to that made by Flaubert's mother about her son: 'Your mania for sentences has dried up your heart.'

Dingley opens during the first weeks of the South African war (in which the French sided with the Boers). The streets of London are full of martial cries; also of recruiting sergeants and the spindly, underfed cockneys whom they target. Dingley observes a scene of entrapment in a tavern, and conceives the idea for a novel in which one such London street-sweeping will be taken up and morally transformed – made a man of – by the experience of military discipline and war. How, though, can Dingley write such a story without first examining the picturesque setting against which his tale will unfold? And so he decides to set off for South Africa, just as Kipling had done – and, for that matter, Arthur Conan Doyle. Kipling went as an observer and propagandist, Doyle as a doctor (though he came back a propagandist); they overlapped for several weeks in the spring of 1900, but appear not to have run into one another.

It's clear that the Tharauds knew a certain amount about Kipling's private life. Thus, they marry their Dingley to an American wife with French blood (Kipling's Caroline Balestier was of Huguenot stock). But whereas Carrie Kipling supported her husband in every word and deed – to the extent that her expressions of military zeal and gloating revenge during the Great War still cast a chill – Mrs Dingley's French blood turns her into the voice of rational dissent and wifely contradictingness. So when Dingley describes the theme of his planned book to her, she proves a robust literary critic: in her opinion, street-sweepings very rarely become heroes. Why, indeed, should a man be morally improved by massacring farmers in a distant land? Surely the experience would make him more, rather than less, of a brute? The novelist dismisses these thoughts as 'the argument of a clergyman – or a Frenchman'. She, in reply, warns him against becoming 'the apostle of a harsh and selfish imperialism'.

The Tharauds find happy mileage in such Anglo-French conflict. They set Dingley up as an exemplar of British imperialism, but also allow into his mouth subtler criticisms of France, and of the failings of the French imperial project. On the voyage out to the Cape (accompanied by his critical wife and their young boy Archie), Dingley falls in with a French journalist whose 'Gascon excitability' provokes the Englishman to the traditional defence of Empire: civilisation not conquest, railways and telegraph not greed and gold. But then he elaborates: 'Are we doing anything more than continuing the project which you French started a couple of hundred years ago and then lost your taste for? It's quite understandable, of course. You prefer to stay at home, and why not? Who would deliberately quit *la belle France*? Whereas we British are the Auvergnats of the world.' (The Auvergnats were by tradition the wandering workers of France, obliged by poverty and poor soil to leave their native province.) The British may be plodders, but what they build lasts; the French specialise only in dash and dazzle. Passing St Helena, Dingley is moved to muse on the career of Napoleon: for all his world-shakingness, the Corsican's ambitions, when set beside the achievements of Disraeli or Cecil Rhodes, had merely been those of an Italian *condottiere*.

As the Dingleys disembark at Cape Town (staying at the Mount Nelson Hotel, just as Kipling had done) the novel becomes both more adventuresome and more serious. Dingley's previous certainties come under threat. For a start, the war is going badly: if the British Army can be outflanked and undermined by a handful of determined Boer farmers, what will become of the Empire? And what will become of Dingley himself? In the presence of real soldiers and real action, he feels himself less than adequate as a man – he is a mere writer, one whose commanding officer, the Muse, is 'an obscure authority, a cowardly and female power'. This is a strikingly accurate prediction of how Kipling was to feel in 1915, when he went to the Western Front as a war correspondent. Though entitled to wear uniform, he declined on the ground that, unlike the troops, he had not earned khaki. Describing his tour of inspection in *France at War*, he specifically invoked the sense of being an inadequate civilian – worse, a writer – in the presence of troops likely to die: 'The soldiers stared, with justified contempt, I thought, upon the civilian who scuttled through their life for a few emotional moments in order to make words out of their blood.'

A trip across the veld to the front line in the company of a photographer, Melton Prior, deepens Dingley's artistic unease. Prior's images of landscape and battlefield are so dismayingly swift and accurate. What will become of Dingley's art if photography deprives him of his key strength, the rendering of the picturesque? Like the rest of his colleagues, he will be reduced to churning out 'psychological novels, French adulteries and Slav moralities'. It is during this upcountry foray that Dingley is recalled to the Cape by news that young Archie has gone down with a fever. Improbably setting off by himself at night-time, he stumbles into an encampment of Boers led by one Lucas du Toit, who turns out to be an old friend and fellow Oxonian (French novelists often seem to believe that everyone in England has been educated at Oxford). Du Toit, on hearing the purpose of Dingley's journey, sends him on his way. This compassionate act points up one of the novel's main themes: pity, its operation and its lack. What matters it that you build an empire if in the process you lose your soul?

Dingley makes it back to the bedside of his son. Young Archie is now pitifully weak, and asks to be diverted with stories. Yet all the stories at Dingley's command cannot save the lad; as he expires, his last delirious words are both an echo and a mockery of his father's militarism: 'Victories,' he wheezes, 'I want victories!' When Archie is buried on a bare hillside near Dossieclipp, 'Dingley felt that with his son he had also buried his finest secret – that of happiness.' Did the Tharauds know when they wrote this line that Kipling had himself lost a child not long before – his daughter Josephine, who succumbed to pneumonia in 1899? Perhaps. But they could not have known that Kipling had reacted in exactly the same way: according to his cousin, the writer Angela Thirkell, much of Rudyard died with his daughter, 'And I have never seen him as a real person since that year.' Still less could the Tharauds have known that in describing the death of a boy made militaristic by his father, they were looking forward to the fate of Kipling's only son John – the moment at which the last remnants of the father's happiness were also extinguished.

Dingley is plunged into crisis by his son's death: just as the Empire can be suddenly derailed by a handful of Boer farmers, so a man's hard-built self-belief can be fractured by the death of a child. The writer's art now appears vain to him, and also lacking: for all its descriptive power and harsh intelligence, there is little in it to refresh the soul. This is a necessary fictional crisis, and perhaps a rather French one, too: while the real Kipling grieved terribly for his two children, he never doubted or despaired of his art – indeed, its austere demands were what kept him functioning. However, it is at this point that readers might begin congratulating themselves on guessing where *Dingley, l'illustre écrivain* is heading. Grief will open its protagonist to pity, and his work will be made richer and truer by this new compassion for humanity. Who knows, perhaps his suffering will lead him to doubt the brassy tootings and hypocritical glories of the Empire?

But the Tharauds were better writers than this. They understood the world – and British imperialism with it. For at this precise moment pity is given a chance to enter Dingley's soul, and it is refused admittance. Lucas du Toit has been taken prisoner and Dingley is asked to intercede. He weighs the demands of friendship and gratitude against the loftier demands of Empire and the pitiless requirements of war. While Mrs Dingley writes pleadingly to the authorities, her husband does nothing except promise a memorial poem; the Boer is shot. Dingley returns to England, and the Tharauds cleverly swerve the plot first one way, then the other. The prideful Dingley writes a newspaper article criticising the war effort in South Africa, calling for conscription (as Kipling did repeatedly) and a Continental army. The newspaper publisher tries to dissuade him, arguing that the nation is not yet ready for such criticism, but Dingley arrogantly insists. Rebuke is immediate and unanimous: readers and critics desert him. In two thousand words he seems to have undone the work of all his twenty previous books. Rejection makes him feel like a 'dispossessed potentate', or a painter going blind (an evident reference to Kipling's novel *The Light That Failed*).

So is this to be the moral of the story? A tale of pride rebuked? Again, the Tharauds surprise us. In a London music hall Dingley watches a cinematic newsreel of the South African war. There are many familiar scenes – including the filmed execution of Lucas du Toit. And he apprehends from the audience's enthusiastic response that when he had withheld pity and assistance from the Boer prisoner, he was in fact deeply in tune with the mood of the British public. So he emerges knowing what he must do – write that novel on the banal yet loyal theme of a miserable cockney transformed by war into a real man. Published as peace is declared – and the women of the East End are doing 'jigs of patriotic indecency' – it proves a 'colossal success'. Nowhere else, in all of his previous books, had 'the Famous Writer expressed with greater pride the egotism of the mother country'.

The novel is thus both a critique of British imperialism – of its coarsening effects, its brutalities and self-deceptions – and a warning against literary populism. But it is also a proper novel about human failure, about the price paid (and the public benefits reaped) when part of the human heart is suppressed. It seems impossible that Kipling could not have heard of *Dingley*; also unlikely he would have read it (not least because of the death of Archie). He seems to have made no recorded reference, public or private, to the novel; fictionalising him, I would imagine silent contempt being his reaction to such Gallic impertinence.

Dingley, l'illustre écrivain was the Tharaud brothers' first and probably greatest success, and they continued their fraternal collaboration on an industrial scale for half a century – their list of titles runs to more than seventy. Jérôme was received into the Académie Française in 1938 after some lengthy debate on the nicely French question of whether half an author could properly occupy a whole seat. The situation was resolved – or, perhaps, doubly complicated – when Jean joined him under the Dôme in 1946. They were, on the basis of *Dingley*, swift and efficient storytellers who, apart from anything else, showed that Kipling, or a version of him, or a part of him, could indeed be given fictional animation. André Gide returned to the subject of the Tharauds in his Journal for 12 July 1921, where he suggested that joint authorship was both their strength and their weakness: 'Everything I have read by the Tharaud brothers has seemed to me of the best quality; the only reproach I think can be made against their books is that they are never dictated by any inner necessity; they do not have those deep and necessary relations with the author in which destiny is pledged.'

Jean died in 1952, Jérôme the following year. Jérôme's seat at the Académie – number 31 – was taken by the ultra-fashionable Jean Cocteau, who ignored the traditional courtesies by saying 'as little as possible' about his predecessor, preferring instead to pay 'ingratiating tribute' to the Académie. It was left to André Maurois, Cocteau's official welcomer, to supply 'the homage to Tharaud which Cocteau had bypassed'. Another half-century later, Cocteau's own dragonfly fame has lost much of its sheen. If the Tharauds are unlikely to enjoy a renaissance, their *Dingley* will survive as more than just a curiosity – as a novel of both seriousness and verve – for some at least of the 'little, little span' that Kipling is borne in mind.

THE WISDOM OF CHAMFORT

CAMUS THOUGHT HIM the most instructive of moralists, and far greater than La Rochefoucauld; Nietzsche and John Stuart Mill revered him; Pushkin read him and allowed Eugene Onegin to do the same; he is an admired presence in the diaries of Stendhal and the Goncourts; Cyril Connolly, another melancholy epicurean with a taste for aphorism, quoted him at length in *The Unquiet Grave*. Yet Nicolas-Sébastien Roch de Chamfort (1741–94) remains virtually unknown in this country.

This is partly our insular fault for not translating enough: the last British edition seems to have been that from the Golden Cockerell Press (550 copies) back in 1926. But perhaps it's also the fault of the genre in which he wrote his only enduring work: the *Maximes et pensées, Caractères et anecdotes, et petits Dialogues philosophiques*. We don't much go for little books of wisdom on these islands. We don't mind table talk, or profound remarks extracted from Boswell's Johnson, or, better still, from novels ('It is a truth universally acknowledged . . .'). But the idea of taking a social or moral observation, polishing it into literary form, and laying it out by itself on a white page as a jeweller lays a sparkler on black velvet – this seems a bit suspicious to us. In some hands, it can seem lordly, snobbish; in others, merely flash.

Take three famous remarks – call them maxims, epigrams, apophthegms as you will. Connolly: 'Imprisoned in every fat man is a thin one wildly signalling to be let out.' Consider the fat men you know. *Every*? *Wildly*? We are not just talking

WeightWatchers here. Is the line, as written, true of many more than the corpulent Connolly himself? Wilde: 'Work is the curse of the drinking classes.' A ritzy, easily made reversal of a common saying. But true? True at all? Or just a look-at-me piece of verbal prestidigitation – one finally as ignorant as it is snooty. La Rochefoucauld: 'There are those who would have never fallen in love had they not first heard love being talked about.' This is much more impressive and authoritative. But, in the end, true? We can all think of people who fall in love 'for the wrong reasons', or who in our view claim to be in love when they aren't; but that isn't what La Rochefoucauld is saying. Again, the contention falls by claiming too much. Life, we might conclude, is rarely a one-liner.

Chamfort is not like this. Camus makes the distinction between the writer of maxims and the moralist. A maxim is like a mathematical equation – its terms are often reversible – and it is no coincidence that the same century, the seventeenth, was in France the great age both of mathematics and of the maxim. But 'all its truth lies within itself, and it no more corresponds to experience than does an algebraic formula'. So much for La Rochefoucauld. Whereas a moralist like Chamfort rarely writes maxims, rarely depends on antithesis and formula. There is little of the Quote of the Week about him. As the Goncourts put it in their journal in 1866, Chamfort is 'way beyond a man of letters penning his reflections. He offers us a condensation of the understanding of the world, the bitter elixir of experience.'

He was born illegitimate in the Auvergne; brains, wit, charm and good looks took him to the heights of Parisian society. He was the friend of Talleyrand, d'Alembert and Helvétius; Mirabeau said that his head was 'electric', and you only had to rub it for it to spark with ideas. He was a familiar of the intellectual salons, and elected to the Académie; Louis XV gave him a pension for a mediocre play which stirred the royal tear ducts. Such straightforward and visible success would have satisfied the normally ambitious; but Chamfort was too intelligent – or too proud, or too self-hating – to be rendered anything as simple as satisfied, let alone happy. His success merely pointed up both his inner contradictions and those of the society which had applauded him. Here is his self-portrait (Reflection 2):

> My whole life is an apparent contradiction of my principles: I dislike monarchy and serve a prince and princess. I am well known for my republican principles yet I have a number of aristocratic friends plastered with royal decorations. I've chosen to be poor and enjoy it, while spending my time with the rich. I despise honours, and yet, when offered, have accepted some. Literature is almost my only consolation but I don't frequent any bright, witty people – nor do I attend sessions of the French Academy. What's more, I think that men need illusions, while having none myself. I consider that passion has more to offer than reason and I no longer feel any sort of passion. Indeed, the list is endless.

This fault line running down the middle is partly what makes Chamfort engaging, human, modern. In his condemnation of human motive he can be as fierce and sarcastic as La Rochefoucauld. But when La Rochefoucauld propounds a system under which self-interest is the impulse for all human activity, the implication remains that La Rochefoucauld himself is somehow exempt from the charge; he is above the moral riff-raff he is anatomising. Chamfort is different in this key respect: his condemnation of humanity includes himself, very specifically. 'If I am anything to go by, man is a foolish animal.'

Wisdom is also more likely to arise from a familiarity with weakness, failure and misery than with strength and wealth. 'It seems to me that, assuming they're both equally

discerning and intelligent, a man born rich will never know
nature, society or the human heart as well as the man who's
poor. The fact is that where the rich man was enjoying himself,
the poor man was finding consolation in thought.' Chamfort
was only poor in comparison to those he frequented; the true
poor usually have no time or energy for the 'consolation of
thought'. But he knew the stigma of illegitimacy; he suffered
disfiguring disease (syphilis, leprosy and elephantiasis have all
been suggested – modern opinion has settled on granuloma-
tosis); and his experience of love was levelling. Having been
a rakish bachelor and part-time misogynist until the great age
of forty, he suddenly fell deeply in love with the wife of a
surgeon, and she with him. Happily, the wife soon became a
widow, whereupon the couple moved to the country to live
out every townee's pastoral idyll. Six months later she died.

A second fault line runs through Chamfort's work – one
whose irony he might have appreciated. Everything he
published in his lifetime, everything by which he made his
name – the plays, the essays, journalism, tributes to literary
greats – has been completely forgotten. Whereas the only
thing he wasn't known for in his lifetime has made his limited
but lasting fame. At some point in the mid-1780s, Chamfort
began jotting down on small bits of paper his conclusions
about life, along with supporting anecdotes, quotations and
scraps of dialogue. There is no indication of what he wrote
when, or of what, if anything, he intended doing with this
accumulation; whether it was to be published, and if so, how
it was to be arranged. Further, between his death and the first
printed selection of his intellectual leavings, many items –
perhaps as many as two thousand – were removed by a person
or persons unknown, presumably on the grounds of being
incriminating or defamatory. As his new translator Douglas
Parmée notes, the result is 'an academic nightmare – and a
paradise for the anthologist, who can juggle them at will'.
Their occasional republication has kept Chamfort's name alive,

though we, as posterity, shouldn't praise ourselves too openly for having the wit to appreciate him. 'Posterity', he wrote, 'merely consists of the opinion of a series of publics. And just look at today's!'

Sainte-Beuve, the most industrious and influential critic of the mid-nineteenth century, judged Chamfort rather harshly: some of his phrases were 'coin which still keeps its value', but many were more like whistling, sharp-tipped arrows. His Reflections were 'horrifying and corrosive'; while his talent was inferior to his wit and his ideas. The moralist had elevated his own isolation and perceived misfortune into a bitter system. When he wrote 'Anyone who's not a misanthrope by the time he's forty has never felt the slightest affection for the human race', it was true 'only for a bachelor'. More generally, Chamfort's supposedly universal conclusions refer only to the highest ranks of a society now long dead. 'Happily, they cease to be true if you look at a less artificial society, one where the sense of family is maintained, and where natural feelings have not been abolished.' For Sainte-Beuve, Chamfort fails the final test of truth.

How to answer the charge of narrowness? First, by pointing out that while representative social samples are a requisite for Gallup polls, they are not necessarily essential for wisdom: are Freud's truths only applicable to the narrow, dead world of Viennese neurotics? Next, we might examine a few of these supposedly localised dicta. Here is one about fame: 'In a country where everyone's keen to show off, many people must, and indeed do, prefer to be a bankrupt rather than be a nobody.' Here is one about status: 'If you want to discover how men are corrupted by their social status, take a look at what they're like in their old age, after long exposure to its influence. Look at old courtiers, judges, lawyers and surgeons, for instance.' And here is one about politics: 'You imagine ministers and other high officials have principles because you've heard them say so. As a result, you avoid asking them to do anything that might cause them to break those principles. However, you soon discover you've been hoodwinked when you see ministers doing things which prove that they're quite unprincipled: it's nothing but a habit they've got into, an automatic reflex.'

Do these seem out-of-date truths? Chamfort quotes Mirabeau to the effect that once a political system has been properly set up, the choice of a particular minister is irrelevant – 'It's like dogs turning a spit, all they need to do is keep their paws moving, their pedigree's unimportant, they don't need to be clever or have a good nose, the spit goes on turning and the meal will be more or less edible.' We can all think of contemporary canine ministers to whom this applies.

Political structures change; political instincts and habits barely develop. Social structures decay and pass; social ambition and techniques of self-advancement continue. Sex and love and their consequences? Chamfort might seem dated and circumscribed in his more than occasional misogyny; and Camus berated him for sharing 'one of the commonest and stupidest sentiments, that is to say a generalised scorn for women'. But – this being Chamfort, and therefore complicated, divided, human – he is also one who observed (almost sentimentally): 'In spite of all the jokes about marriage, I can't see what anyone can say against a man of sixty who marries a woman of fifty-six.' And could the following insight into love be made by a man who was merely a bachelor, or merely a misogynist? 'In love, everything is both true and false; it's the one subject on which it's impossible to say anything absurd.' Chamfort is various, contradictory, but always stimulating, never one to flatter the reader's complacency; and while there are dicta to quarrel with, there are very few to which the response will be, 'That's just not true – wasn't true then, isn't true now.' One of my favourite lines is also aimed, you feel, at the author himself: 'Having lots of ideas doesn't mean you're clever, any more than having lots of soldiers means you're a good general.'

Camus, without naming Sainte-Beuve, deals with the charge of narrowness rather differently. Yes, he says, Chamfort was writing about a social elite; but no, he wasn't generalising about the whole race from that narrow basis. The true moralist – as opposed to the maker of maxims – is an observer of human particularity in the same way as a novelist is. Hence the Reflections are 'a kind of disorganised novel', 'an unadmitted novel', 'a satirical novel'. Indeed, 'if you could only restore to the work the coherence which the author declined to give it, you would have something far superior to the collection of pensées than it appears to be'.

This is a generous and imaginative (and slightly overstated) claim, which indicates well the broader nature of Chamfort's work. The Reflections contain long-pondered conclusions about human nature and behaviour, but also anecdotes, stories, brief character descriptions, and jokes. (Reflection 67: 'The most misspent day in any life is the one when you've failed to laugh.') This is what gives the book its tone and texture; also the sense of an author addressing a reader. Chamfort the shadow novelist wants to share his wisdom with us, but he also wants to share his gossip:

Louis XV said to one of his mistresses: 'You've been to bed with all my subjects.'
    'Oh, Your Majesty!'
    'You've had the Duc de Choiseul.'
    'He's so powerful . . .'
    'Maréchal de Richelieu.'
    'He's so witty . . .'
    'Manville.'
    'He has such lovely legs . . .'
    'And what about the Duc d'Aumont, who hasn't got any of these fine qualities?'
    'Oh sire, he's so devoted to Your Majesty!'

Chamfort's ambivalence about the society whose acclaim he had sought led first to periods of withdrawal and philosophical seclusion; later, to support for the organised rejection of that society known as the Revolution. Though this might seem logical as well as principled, his detailed motivation is less clear. Chateaubriand was astonished that someone with such a deep understanding of humankind could end up embracing any cause. Sainte-Beuve's theory was that Chamfort's mortal grudge against the *ancien régime* was at bottom literary: it had judged him to be merely a nice young poet, and had patronisingly treated him as such. Connolly pointed to the 'temperament of a love-child', which produced both a great need for love and 'that equally violent feeling, so familiar to bastards, of a grievance against society'.

Whichever motive we prefer, it led to 'The Predicament of Chamfort', as Connolly called it in *The Unquiet Grave*:

> His predicament is one with which we are all familiar . . . that of the revolutionary whose manners and way of life are attached to the old regime, whose ideals and loyalties belong to the new, and who by a kind of courageous exhibitionism is impelled to tell the truth about both, and to expect from the commissars of King Stork the same admiration for his sallies as they received from the courtiers of King Log.

When the Revolution broke out, Chamfort sided with his friend Mirabeau; he spoke at street corners, coined popular slogans ('War upon the chateaux, peace upon the cottages'), and was one of the first to enter the stormed Bastille. He supported the Revolution longer and harder than others of his kind: 'Do you imagine you can make revolutions to the smell of rose water?' he asked one waverer. But his independent habit of mind did not desert him. When the Jacobin slogan 'Fraternity or death!' was being chalked on walls, he knew politics and human nature well enough to reformulate it without the spin: 'Be my brother or I'll kill you.'

It was not long before King Stork dipped his bill. Chamfort was denounced, imprisoned, released, and threatened with fresh arrest; deciding to take the philosopher's way out, he put a pistol to his head. But all he succeeded in doing was to smash his nose and put out his right eye. Then he took a razor – or in some accounts a knife – and hacked at his throat, wrists and ankles, before collapsing in a pool of blood which streamed under the door. Amazingly, he survived, and characteristically complained that poverty had yet again undone him: 'Seneca was rich, he had everything he needed, including a warm bath to do it in, and the best of surroundings, whereas I'm just a poor devil who can't afford any of that . . . Still, at least I've got a bullet in my head, that's the main thing.' It was and it wasn't; indeed, he seemed on the way to recovery when the maladroitness of a doctor did for him. His last words were: 'I am leaving this world in which the heart must either break, or else turn to bronze.' True? Partly true? Not at all true? Discuss.

THE MAN WHO SAVED OLD FRANCE

———◆———

I FIRST STARTED GOING to France almost fifty years ago, on motoring holidays with my parents and brother. The towns and villages we then visited – quaintly, they were still filled with nothing but French people – had a solid, unchanging feel to them and a recognisable morphology: from smart *mairie* and *PTT* to dilapidated *lavoir* and rank *pissoir*, from war memorial listing unforgotten dead to blank walls pasted with the huge words 'DEFENSE D'AFFICHER – LOI DU 29 JUILLET 1881' (a proclamation far more strident than the flyers it was designed to deter). Behind this ordinary, diurnal France, giving it wider and deeper meaning, was the monumental France to which my schoolteacher parents introduced me (at times, inflicted upon me): the chateaux and cathedrals, museums and public buildings, artworks and ruins – a France of history, power and money, a France of official, national beauty. There seemed an extraordinary amount of it around, its symbols leaping out from every fold of the yellow Michelin road map. A back-seat navigator, I would prepare my parents for what lay round the next bend. A solid black oblong denoted a chateau worth slowing down for; a similar oblong with legs at each corner one worth a stop; a triangle of black dots meant a ruined castle; while a curious mark, like a wonky version of the pi symbol, indicated some prehistoric vestige. All this seemed just as solid and eternal as the daily life, if not more so.

When we toured the chateaux of the Loire, I couldn't help noticing that many of these great palaces seemed remarkably empty of furniture, and was given to understand that it had all disappeared in the Revolution. Into my mind came vague images – perhaps culled from the film of *A Tale of Two Cities* – of looting sans-culottes with wild eyes and bad shaves. The green Michelin guidebooks to which we referred for our facts were, I now realise, written and edited by a team diplomatically keen not to offend any strand of French opinion; so there was much elision, and a tactical unwillingness to take any controversial (or even discernible) side in France's long internecine history. Nor did the books indicate how precarious had been the earlier life of this solid monumentality we dutifully visited. Still less did they mention, let alone salute, the man without whose decisive influence and actions what the French now call their patrimony would have been considerably diminished: Prosper Mérimée.

On this side of the Channel, Mérimée (1803–70) is mainly remembered as the author of the novella from which *Carmen* was drawn; though Bizet's opera, in the words of Mérimée's best British biographer, Alan Raitt, is 'no more than an emasculated and prettified version of Mérimée's tale'. He wrote fiction – specialising in themes of cruelty, revenge and the Implacable Woman – plays and poetry. He was a serious Anglophile, who once proposed marriage to Mary Shelley, and was so well known at the British Museum that the guards used to salute him when he arrived; he was also passionate about Spain, and in later life a Russophile who translated Pushkin, Turgenev and Gogol. He was a traveller, a courtier, an Academician, friend of Stendhal, lover of George Sand, truffler of the sexual lowlife, and a senator under Napoleon III. But his true, if largely forgotten, claim to enduring fame is as the second Inspector General of Historic Monuments, a post he occupied from 1834 to 1860.

There had been previous attempts to catalogue and protect France's architectural history, most of them either compromised or half-hearted. If the French Revolution had been at times revengefully destructive, it also introduced for the first time the idea of officially conserving works of art and architecture. So each decree of confiscation also included a demand for protection: these buildings, these paintings, these tapestries were now in the care of the people. Between 1790 and 1795 there was a Commission of Monuments, set up to make an inventory, with the help of regional correspondents, of all that was worth preserving. Although what was worth preserving above all was the Revolution itself, and when it came under attack from counter-revolutionaries and foreign armies, there was much patriotic handing in of silver, gold, rich cloth, vases, and so on. Bronze statuary was melted down, while the lead roof of Chartres Cathedral was stripped off in Year III on the grounds that 'our prime concern is to crush our enemies'. The Commission hoped to protect the royal tombs at Saint-Denis – 'not out of love for them, but for the sake of history and the philosophic idea'. But the Convention, intent upon expunging the very idea of monarchy, authorised the destruction of 'these monuments to pride and flattery'. Since what later becomes a nation's patrimony (and its list of tourist attractions) normally starts off as just such vainglorious display, it is fortunate this principle was not more widely applied.

Kings nevertheless returned to France, and it was with the bourgeois monarchy of Louis-Philippe, brought in by the 'Three Glorious Days' of July 1830, that the protection of the nation's patrimony became an urgent matter, supported at the highest levels. Ludovic Vitet, appointed the first Inspector General of Historic Monuments, defined his task as to make an inventory of all buildings which 'because of their date, their architecture, or the events to which they have borne witness, merit the attention of the archaeologist, the artist and the historian'. Such listing was clearly a massive task: Mérimée drily observed that it would probably take 250 years and require 900 volumes of illustration to go with the text. But it was also a thrilling, generous idea – 'administrative romanticism', in one expert's nice phrase – typical of the new generation which came into power in 1830. Sainte-Beuve later wrote: 'It was like a kind of pilgrimage. Experts combed the provinces, rushing towards any town which had a steeple pointing like a finger into the sky, towards every church tower and Gothic arch. They hunted through the oldest parts of towns, explored the narrowest alleyways, and stopped dead at any piece of incised or decorated stonework.'

This surge of enthusiasm came from several sources. First, a panicky realisation that chunks of France were just being demolished, carted away, broken up. The principled (or vindictive) hostility of Revolutionaries to the property of Aristocracy and Church had given way to pragmatic recycling by builders who treated ancient monuments as quarries, and antiquarians who rounded up loot to sell abroad. In April 1819 the Minister of the Interior asked Prefects to report on the most important buildings in their *départements* 'in order to prevent them being dismantled and taken away by the English'. Victor Hugo declared '*Guerre aux démolisseurs!*' – War on the Vandals – and wrote in 1825: 'There are two things about a historic building: its use and its beauty. Its use is a matter for its owner, but its beauty belongs to everybody. So an owner goes beyond his rights in knocking it down.' This was a less politicised – though still militant – version of the Revolution's declaration of public ownership. Hugo gave further, fictional impetus to his campaign with the novel *Notre-Dame de Paris* (1831), in which the cathedral becomes as vivid a character as Quasimodo himself.

What the thieving English wanted was Gothic, being themselves in full Revival mode. The French came later to the rediscovery of Gothic, but with a deeper national purpose. Gothic was held to be the authentic architecture of France, whereas Classicism was a foreign interpolation. Viollet-le-Duc, who began as Mérimée's protégé, and later became the most famous architect and restorer in nineteenth-century France, wrote that 'Our country is closer to medieval France than to classical Rome. Our religion and our climate have remained the same. The building materials have also remained the same, and we would feel more at home in a thirteenth-century French mansion than in any palace of Lucullus.' Gothic was patriotic; Gothic also best expressed the Catholicism which was now back in fashion.

But there was a political aspect to the new regime's enthusiasm for ancient monuments. The July Monarchy had no real legitimacy, so it needed to confect one. In rebranding the country it therefore claimed to represent both new and old: to draw on France's recent revolutionary heritage, but also to annex the idea of Ancient France, now being rediscovered and properly valued. Though there was a potential problem here: if you identified your new regime with a collection of collapsed and collapsing edifices, what sort of a message was that sending out? So the concept of not just protection but restoration was both vital and symbolic. The rediscovered heritage was to be presented once again as the restorer knew – or guessed, or hoped – it originally had been. In the old days, if a church had a broken twelfth-century capital, it would have been mended with one in a contemporary style – thirteenth, fourteenth, fifteenth century, or whatever. Now, in the second quarter of the nineteenth century, the notion of reimagining, and then attempting to transport, a building back to its original state was for the first time introduced on a wide scale. This was not to prove a simple matter.

Mérimée was still only thirty when appointed to succeed Vitet on 17 May 1834. He had a broad general grounding in the arts (his father was perpetual secretary at the École des Beaux-Arts, his mother an accomplished portrait painter), but was inexperienced in archaeology. Alexandre Dumas commented sardonically that Mérimée would have to begin by learning what he would then be expected to teach others. But he did learn, and quickly. On appointment, he told his English friend Sutton Sharpe that 'the job fits my tastes and temperament perfectly: it appeals to both my idleness and my love of travel'. But there was little idleness about the new Inspector General. Only six weeks into the job, he set off for the south of France on what was the first of a series of annual tours of inspection. Each summer for the next eighteen years, he would criss-cross the country for weeks and months, examining and reporting, chivvying and condemning. The roads were bad, the coaches uncomfortable, the inns bug-ridden, the food often inedible, the women (and Mérimée was very keen on women) often implacably virtuous, and the local experts at times dunce-like. Mérimée's private letters are full of wry exasperation:

> The truth is that the life I lead is absolutely exhausting. When I'm not travelling around by coach, I get up at nine, have breakfast, then give audience to librarians, archivists and the like. They take me to look at their wretched ruins, and if I say they aren't Carlovingian, they look on me as a blackguard and start intriguing with the local deputy to get my salary reduced. Caught between conscience and self-interest, I tell them their monument is marvellous and that there's nothing in the north to compare with it. Then they invite me to dinner, and the local paper says I'm the devil of a clever fellow. They beg me to inscribe a sublime thought in an album; I obey with a shudder. At the end of the evening, they ceremoniously escort me back to my hotel, which prevents me from indulging in vice. I go back to my room worn out and sit up putting together notes, drawings, official letters, etc. I wish those who envy me could see me then.

Mérimée certainly found some of the local antiquaries comically cocky – when in doubt, they fell back on classifying things as 'Phoenician' – and some of the architects profoundly ignorant: the man at Béziers was 'the biggest ass ever to hold a drawing-pen', the one at Saint-Savin 'a man quite without education and remarkably stupid'. Some of the provincial officials were obstructive, and some of the clergy proprietorial: the curé at Chauvigny, Mérimée noted with astonishment, insisted 'that the church belonged to him'. But the Inspector General would have made little headway if he had been heavy-handed, or bossily Parisian. He was not just extraordinarily industrious, knowledgeable and incorruptible; he was also charming and persuasive. Viollet-le-Duc, who travelled with him on several of his tours, wrote: 'Without even noticing what was happening, the person to whom he was speaking was induced to give him all the information he wanted, and confess everything to him. He would have made the most amiable examining magistrate one could imagine. At the same time, he was a good diplomat and a clever politician.'

He had to be; not least because he and his Commission had little more than moral authority. The fact of listing a monument (1,076 were put on the roll in 1840; nearly 4,000 by 1849) did not give it any legal protection. If an owner knocked a building down, or a municipality decided on a piece of street-widening to the detriment of some awkward medieval vestige, there was nothing Paris could do about it: the necessary protective laws were not finally introduced until 1887–9, nearly two decades after Mérimée's death. So his role was part aesthetic expert, part moral presence, part patriotic cheerleader. When Guizot, the Interior Minister, described the job of Inspector General in 1830, he not only drew its terms very widely (museums, private collections and manuscripts were included as well as buildings and works of art) but announced the hortatory principle which was to infuse it. The task of an Inspector General, he wrote, was to 'stimulate the zeal' of local authorities, 'so that no building of incontestable merit would be lost through either ignorance or collapse'.

This collaboration with departmental and municipal authorities was desirable for democratic reasons, and necessary for economic ones. Only one listing in three led to state funding; so the intention was also to stir local pride in the monument, and release local money.

What Mérimée discovered, as he went on his annual rounds, was that much of France's monumental patrimony was in a state of near-collapse. The roof of Chartres Cathedral was on the point of falling in; the wall paintings at Saint-Savin – the largest array of medieval frescoes in France, and possibly Europe – had been crudely obliterated with whitewash; a few days after Mérimée had inspected the Vice-Regent's tower, 'one of the most ancient edifices in Avignon', it simply fell down. Symbolic of much elsewhere was the condition of the great abbey church at Vézelay. Its left-hand tower had been pulled down by Protestants in 1569; the Revolution had hacked off offending bas-reliefs; and then, 'as if to prove that the nineteenth century did not yield to the past in the matter of vandalism', the Army Corps of Engineers, engaged in mapping the country, had built 'a ridiculous octagonal observatory' right on top of the remaining tower. Walls had fallen in, or were rotting away from damp; trees were growing out of the stonework; the vaulting could scarcely hold together any longer; and as Mérimée sat in the church sketching the grim scene, stones from the roof kept falling all around him. The town itself, with only a thousand inhabitants and no significant industry, didn't have money enough even to stabilise the church in its current morbid condition. 'So things get worse by the day,' Mérimée wrote in his report to the minister. 'If we delay our support any longer, the church will become so dangerous that we shall have to pull it down.'

Nor was it merely Time and History that were assailing the patrimony. Theft, vandalism and self-interested urban development were happening by the week. The famous Roman mausoleum outside Saint-Rémy may be eighteen metres high;

but shortly before Mérimée inspected it in October 1834, 'an Englishman' (if in doubt blame *les Rosbifs*) managed to scale it in the middle of the night and make off with the heads of the two draped figures from the very top. In Avignon, Corsican soldiers billeted in the Palais des Papes supplemented their pay by chipping off the medieval frescoes and selling them; while a horticultural entrepreneur had taken over the city's famous bridge, planting almond trees and cabbages along it. In La Charité-sur-Loire, two locksmiths had built their houses against the wall of the abbey church, so that their sleeping alcoves were decorated with spectacular eleventh- and twelfth-century bas-reliefs. A month before Mérimée's arrival, a soldier had lodged with one of the locksmiths and slept next to a sculpture of God the Father surrounded by saints and angels. He had a less than satisfactory night. In the morning he took his stick, chastised the figure of God with the words, 'You invented bedbugs, so this one is for you,' and knocked its head off.

There was also institutional vandalism to contend with. Historic buildings were now being used as storehouses, shops, stables and beer halls. The Palais des Papes was a barracks, Noirlac Abbey a china factory. Since the Revolution, the church of St-Étienne in Strasbourg had been used first as a music hall, later as a tobacco warehouse. Saint Savinien at Poitiers was a prison, and its choir a padded cell: the Inspector General was faced with a request to destroy the interior's few remaining sculptures of worth, to stop the inmates treating them as climbing stones and making their escape. Mérimée's task was rarely helped by other government bodies: he found the Ministry of Ecclesiastical Affairs obstructive, the Ministry of Works destructive, and the Ministry of War 'the biggest vandal in France'. Near Carnac, road builders, unwilling to make a detour of a few metres, smashed 'the beautiful menhirs of Erdeven' to powder. The city of Orléans pulled down its old Hôtel-Dieu. At Bourges, the richly late-Gothic Maison de Jacques Coeur had been turned into a courtroom, a change of use which wrecked the internal layout and decoration. Mérimée judged it impossible to restore the interior to its original condition, because it would mean that 'we would be obliged to *invent*'. He was constantly faced with such decisions, and expressed his principles in the dictum: 'It is better to consolidate than repair, better to repair than restore, better to restore than embellish, and in no circumstances knock down.'

Yet worse than individual or institutional vandalism was something less immediately obvious, indeed paradoxical: the mutilations inflicted by wrong-headed restorers. Of all the enemies Mérimée faced, bad restoration was the one which obsessed and infuriated him most. 'I have no hesitation in saying that neither the iconoclastic fury of Protestantism nor the stupid vandalism of the Revolution has left such deplorable marks on our monuments as the bad taste of the eighteenth and nineteenth centuries. The barbarians at least used to leave ruins; the so-called repairers' have left us only their own sorry work.' Medieval frescoes were whitewashed out; crude new oil painting made churches look like taverns; old stone was brutally scraped away at until it matched the colour of the new stone with which it had been patched. At Bayeux they installed proud new stained glass which was nothing but 'a gaudy and pretentious pastiche'. At Saint-Savin, one of the buildings closest to his heart, the Inspector General was moved to rage by the enthusiastic repainting and filling-in of the frescoes: 'the most revolting sight in the world', he called it. The colours were luridly modern; there was a grotesque portrait of God the Father 'squinting horribly', plus an eagle of St John the Apostle looking more 'like a cockerel'. Within an hour Mérimée had this destructive restoration effaced.

It is amazing that, with all these enemies, he kept both his sanity and his stamina. 'I am already at war with so many towns', he wrote in the 1840s, 'that one more or less doesn't worry me much.' Given that the Commission had only moral and persuasive authority, there were inevitable defeats and losses – some of which occurred after a building had supposedly been saved. The state might list a church, restore it at considerable expense, and hand it back, only for the community to finish the job wreckingly. As the architectural historian Paul Léon put it in his magisterial *La Vie des monuments français*, 'Their barbarous ignorance often succeeded in removing from the edifice its entire value as a work of art.' When Mérimée reported on Carpentras in September 1834, he described a delightfully walled and fortified town, like a junior version of Avignon. Despite his praise, when he returned eleven years later, the town had pulled down the better, southern ramparts, and was hard at work destroying the rest. 'You wouldn't recognise the place,' Mérimée wrote to Vitet. 'It's now the filthiest and vilest dump you could imagine.' Avignon similarly wanted to sacrifice its ramparts to facilitate the railway line, whose course would also have chopped through the famous old bridge – a piece of vandalism that was successfully resisted.

It's true that the school of architect-restorers brought into existence by Mérimée and his Commission did not always follow his careful and properly austere precepts. At Blois the architect Duban, 'seeking a public success', commissioned an equestrian statue of Louis XII, plus all sorts of balustrades, ornaments and window framings – rank embellishments and inventions. Viollet-le-Duc – especially after 1860, when Mérimée's direct influence waned – increasingly produced fully reinvented medievalism: the brand-new old. Knowledgeable tourists of a later generation, like Henry James (in 1882) and Edith Wharton (in 1908), loathed much of what he did. They much preferred evocative and crumbling old piles. As Wharton wrote: 'How much more eloquently these tottering stones tell their story, how much deeper into the past they take us, than the dapper weather-tight castles – Pierrefonds, Langeais, and the rest – on which the arch-restorer has worked his will, reducing them to mere museum specimens, archaeological toys, from which all the growths of time have been ruthlessly stripped!'

Mérimée was well aware of the dangers of reinventing the past, though he sometimes kept a diplomatic silence. Viollet-le-Duc had made his name by saving Vézelay and restoring Carcassonne in a way that pleased even Edith Wharton; but increasingly he tended to rely on his own imagination. The chateau of Pierrefonds was given a 'riotous treatment' by Viollet at the command of the Empress Eugénie, who later asked Mérimée what he thought of it. 'It is a piece of work', he replied, 'before which I feel utterly crushed.' The Empress, not reading the ambiguity, replied, 'Thank you, you are a true friend.'

In the 1840s, Mérimée wrote that 'the job of an inspector of Historic Monuments is to be a voice crying in the wilderness'; but his voice resounded through that century and beyond. A French critic of the 1920s noted the paradoxical turn of his life. He had been 'a young man who had put everything into trying to write like Voltaire and dress like Beau Brummell, yet who became the most diligent of bureaucrats and the most zealous of archaeologists'. A further paradox was that this convinced atheist, who had not even been baptised, was responsible for saving large numbers of ecclesiastical buildings – first from falling down, and then from the bright decorative vandalism of know-nothing restorers and proprietorial clergy. Paul Léon, summing up Prosper Mérimée's achievements, wrote that 'Thanks to him the cathedrals of Laon and Vézelay and the Abbey of Saint-Savin are still standing, and towns like Caen, Avignon, Cunault, Saulieu and Narbonne are still dressed in their finery of great monuments'. Modern tourists, seeing that distant spire pointing to the heavens, spotting the glisten of pepper-pot towers half lost in woodland, or gazing up at the ribbed vaulting of an airy abbey, should pause and give thanks to the man without whom one French town after another might have ended up looking like Carpentras.

And yes, I have been to Carpentras. And all I can remember is the pizza I ate there.

THE PROFILE OF FÉLIX FÉNÉON

IN 1880, THE neo-Impressionist Paul Signac offered to paint Félix Fénéon, the very coiner, four years previously, of the term 'neo-Impressionist'. The critic-subject responded with model evasiveness, and then a proviso: 'I will express only one opinion: effigy absolutely full-face – do you agree?' Signac did not agree. Five months later, the best-known image of Félix Fénéon emerged: in left profile, holding top hat and cane, presenting a lily to an off-canvas recipient (homage to an artist? love-gift to a woman?) against a circusy pinwheel of dashing pointillist colour. Fénéon, whether from vanity or critic's pique at the artist's disobedience, strongly disliked the image, commenting that 'the portraitist and the portrayed had done one another a cruel disservice'. He accepted the picture, however, and kept it on his walls until Signac died some forty-five years later. But neither that event, nor the passing of time, mellowed his judgement: in 1943 he told his friend and future literary executor, the critic Jean Paulhan, that it was 'the least successful work painted by Signac'.

Worse for Fénéon, it established a template of profilism. Bonnard, Vuillard and Vallotton all depicted him in more or less the same pose: leaning forwards – bent into a near-impossible arrowhead in Vuillard's rendition – at his desk at the *Revue Blanche*, with left profile and monkish tonsure on display. Toulouse-Lautrec and van Dongen followed suit. Fénéon may not have liked it, but it was the more interesting view. In full face he looks as if he might be someone else: in old age he resembled Gide. Whereas the profile shot offered artists much more promising material: a big bony nose, prominent chin and, beneath it, the flowing tuft of a goatee. Highly individual, yet also, somehow, generic. This angle made people think of Uncle Sam or Abraham Lincoln (Apollinaire called him 'a faux Yankee'); also of the Moulin Rouge dancer Valentin le Désossé, for whom he was sometimes mistaken. 'We had, it seems,' he admitted, 'analogies that were flattering to neither of us.'

But this profilism was also psychologically and aesthetically accurate: a representation of Fénéon's obliqueness, his decision not to face us directly, either as readers or as examiners of his life. In literary and artistic history he comes down to us in shards, kaleidoscopically. Luc Sante, in his introduction to *Novels in Three Lines*, describes him well as being 'invisibly famous' – and he was even more invisible to anglophone readers until Joan Ungersma Halperin's fine study of him appeared in 1988. Art critic, art dealer, owner of the best eye in Paris as the century turned, promoter of Seurat, the only gallerist Matisse ever trusted; journalist, ghostwriter for Colette's Willy, literary adviser then chief editor of the *Revue Blanche*; friend of Verlaine, Huysmans and Mallarmé, publisher of Laforgue, editor and organiser of Rimbaud's *Les Illuminations*; translator of both Joyce and *Northanger Abbey*. He was invisible partly because he was a facilitator rather than a creator, but also because of his manner, which was elliptical, ironic, taciturn. Some found him caustic and rather frightening; though his actions were often kindly. Valéry called him 'just, pitiless and gentle'. The Goncourt *Journal* reports the verdict of the poet Henri de Régnier: 'a real original, born in Italy and looking like an American. An intelligent man who is trying to turn himself into a character and impress people with his epigrams . . . But a man of heart, goodness and sensitivity, belonging wholly to the world of the eccentric, the disfavoured, the down-and-out.'

For thirteen years, he worked at the War Office, rising to the position of chief clerk. Frenchly, he managed to combine this with being a committed anarchist, by both word and deed. He supported the cause as journalist, editor and – almost certainly – bomb-planter. In 1894 he was arrested in a sweep of anarchists and charged under the kind of catch-all law which governments panicked by terror attacks stupidly tend to enact. Part of the evidence against him was that a police search of his office had turned up a vial of mercury and a matchbox containing eleven detonators. Fénéon added to the history of implausible excuses by claiming that his father, who had recently died and was therefore unavailable to corroborate his evidence, had found them in the street. His defence was paid for by the artistic maecenas Thadée Natanson, and he seems to have enjoyed matching his mind against the lawyers. When the presiding judge put it to him that he had been spotted talking to a known anarchist behind a gas lamp, he replied coolly, 'Can you tell me, Monsieur le Président, which side of a gas lamp is its behind?' This being France, wit did him no disservice with the jury, and he was acquitted. The following year, Wilde was to discover the downside of courtroom wit. Strangely, this was also the year in which Lautrec painted the two victims side by side – and in profile, naturally – as spectators at the Moulin Rouge.

The trial was the high point in Fénéon's visibility. For the next half-century he became gradually more elusive. He never published a book, restricting himself to the 43-page monograph *Les Impressionistes en 1886*. This came out in an edition of 227 copies, and he declined all subsequent offers to reprint it. His journalism proceeded from full byline to initials to total anonymity. A publisher once invited him to write his memoirs; naturally he refused. Another suggested bringing out the *Nouvelles en trois lignes*; he replied angrily, 'I aspire only to silence.' A reply on a par with that of his near-contemporary,

the Swiss writer Robert Walser, who was once visited in the
lunatic asylum to which he had retreated by a friend who
asked how his work was coming along. 'I'm not here to write,'
replied Walser, 'but to be mad.'

Fénéon's elusiveness infected the way others wrote about
him. The biographical note in the Pléiade edition of Jules
Renard's *Journal* takes up more space than the two entries
devoted to him, one of which reads simply: 'Fénéon's goatee.'
Mallarmé was a close friend who stood as a character witness
at his trial. But here is the poet writing to his near-miss
mistress Méry Laurent immediately after the event: 'My poor
friend Fénéon (no, he has a very interesting physiognomy)
has been acquitted and this gives me happiness. The fruit has
not yet arrived or been eaten. The ham reigns supreme and
Geneviève considers we put it in its trousers (the bag) too
soon after the meal.' This is all part of the same paragraph.
The great public crisis of Fénéon's life is subsumed into the
more important matter of food. Though Fénéon might well
have approved, especially of the phrase 'the ham reigns
supreme'.

The *Nouvelles en trois lignes*, now translated into English
for the first time, is not, in any normal sense, a book, if
that word implies authorial intent. In 1906, Fénéon worked
for the newspaper *Le Matin*, and for some months was
assigned to compose the *faits divers* column – known in
hackdom as *chiens écrasés* (run-over dogs). He had at his
disposal the wire services, local and provincial newspapers,
and communications from readers. He composed up to
twenty of these three-line fillers in the course of his evening
shift. They were printed – unsigned, of course – and read
for a quick smile or breath-intake or head-shake, and then
forgotten. They would not have been identifiable from the
general mass of *faits divers* had not Fénéon's mistress, Camille
Plateel, dutifully cut out his contributions – all 1,220 of
them – and stuck them in an album (his wife apparently

did the same). Jean Paulhan then discovered and published them. It is an interesting position, to be the literary executor of a writer who aspired only to silence and resolutely refused publication in his lifetime. Paulhan duly brought out this unintended, unauthored, unshaped, unofficial 'book', and Fénéon's underground literary reputation started to go overground.

Sartre, writing about Renard's *Journal*, described the dilemma of the French prose writer at the end of the nineteenth century. The great descriptive and critical project that had been the realist novel – from Flaubert via Goncourt and Maupassant to Zola – had run its course, had sucked up the world and left little for the next generation of practitioners. The only way forward lay through compression, annotation, pointillism. In a grand and rather grudging tribute to Renard, Sartre wrote that the *Journal* 'is at the origin of many more modern attempts to seize the essence of the single thing'. Gide, whose own journal overlapped for many years with Renard's, complained – perhaps rivalrously – that the latter's was 'not a river but a distillery'.

Renard – who also features in Bonnard's drawing of the *Revue Blanche* offices – distilled; Fénéon went further and barely bottled a drop. Sante calls this 'an aggressive silence, as charged, dense and reverberating as Malevich's black canvas. It affirms that all writing is compromise, that conception will always trump execution, that ego and politics are everyone's co-authors. It may be rooted in despair but it grows in the direction of transcendence. It wishes to free poetry from books and release it into daily life.' These rather grand claims provoke two immediate responses: first, that Malevich's black canvas did at least exist; and, second, that if such was indeed the intention behind the writer's silence, then what is the quality of disobedience in the actions, first of Paulhan, and then of Sante?

In 1914, Apollinaire started a wider awareness of the

Nouvelles en trois lignes by claiming, in a newspaper column – appropriately anonymous – that they had 'invented' the 'words at liberty adopted by the Futurists'. Their clandestine reputation and significance has, over the century, become an *idée reçue*. Here it is, as related by Hilary Spurling in her biography of Matisse: 'For years [*sic*] he also wrote a national newspaper column, consisting entirely of more or less offbeat items collected from the press and retailed with a terse, disconcerting wit which raised the news round-up to a proto-Surrealist art form.' Sante has further claims: that the *Nouvelles* 'depict the France of 1906 in its full breadth'; that they have the perfection of haikus; that they are 'Fénéon's *Human Comedy*'; that they have the same essence as the pointillists' adamantine dots; that they are like random photographs found in a trunk; that they parallel Braque and Picasso's use of newspaper in cubist collage; finally, that they 'represent a crucial, if hitherto overlooked milestone in the history of modernism'. The publishers, for good measure, throw in Andy Warhol.

To begin at the beginning: they are *nouvelles en trois lignes*. The news in three lines, laid out in *Le Matin* under the subheads of Parisian Suburbs, *Départements* (i.e. provincial stories) and Foreign. These attributions are not maintained in Sante's edition; but then they were probably not evident from Camille Plateel's scrapbook. Fénéon had previous experience of forms demanding compression and permitting irony. In 1886 he had been one of four co-authors who produced – in three days flat – a *Petit Bottin des lettres et des arts*, with cheeky and whimsical definitions of cultural notables. Later, as an anarchist journo in the 1890s, he had directed his sarcasm at more serious targets:

> Dead sick of himself after reading the book by Samuel Smiles (*Know Thyself*), a judge just drowned himself at Coulange-la-Vineuse. If only this excellent book could be read throughout the magistracy.

Or:

> A policeman, Maurice Marullas, has blown out his
> brains. Let's save the name of this honest man from
> being forgotten.

This was to be very much the style of the *Nouvelles en trois
lignes* a decade later, even if the political opinions were now
to be held back.

'The original French of the title', Sante writes, 'can mean
either "the news in three lines" or "novellas in three lines".'
It would, of course, only have meant the first when the newspaper named the column; and *nouvelles* normally means 'short
stories' in French. Even allowing for the slipperiness of fictional
taxonomy, it's a considerable stretch to make it mean 'novellas',
and a completely impossible stretch to make it mean 'novels'.
But *Novels in Three Lines* is a more sexily paradoxical title. If
'all writing is compromise', what does that make publishing?

Most of the thousand or so items here (Sante has omitted
154 on the grounds of obscurity) tell of violence in one form
or another. Here are murder, suicide and rape; anarchist bombs
and acid attacks; theft, arson and poisonings; the discharge,
accidental or deliberate, of a wide range of firearms; runnings-
down by train, carriage, horse, automobile and bus. Suicide
– sometimes in pact form – may come by hanging, poisoning,
incineration, railway line, river or well. Rabies attacks the
human body, while strikes attack the economic and social
body. There are weird eccentricities, bathetic failures, hoaxes
and scams of impressive originality:

> 'Ouch!' cried the cunning oyster-eater. 'A pearl!'
> Someone at the next table bought it for 100 francs.
> It had cost 30 cents at the dime store.

What there is very little of – unsurprisingly, given the
tradition of the *faits divers* column – is normality (and therefore

breadth, Balzacian or otherwise). Only two areas suggest this: considerable space is given to the mildest happenings in the French navy, often involving small amounts of damage to tiller and hull; and there is a strange but consistent interest in the election of May queens.

There are certain givens to this journalistic format. You must mention names, places, ages and, if possible, professions; summarise the newsworthy event; and indicate motive, if known, or guessable, or inventable. All this in three lines. Sometimes this results in a car-crash of mere names:

> A case of revenge: near Monistrol-d'Allier, M. Blanc and M. Boudoissier were killed and mutilated by M. Plet, M. Pascal and M. Gazanion.

Trades and professions – especially if far from those of the newspaper's readers – provide points of colour: here are chestnut vendors, ragpickers and resin-tappers. Sometimes these opposing trades clash:

> In the military zone, in the course of a duel over scrawny Adeline, basket-weaver Capello stabbed bear-baiter Monari in the abdomen.

Had the bear-baiter stabbed the basket-weaver, it might have been less unusual; that it happened in the military zone makes it more piquant; that the surnames imply the hot blood of the south, and that Adeline was scrawny – whether she was or not in reality is almost beside the point – make it into a miniature story.

Only very occasionally do these stories join up to create a thread of narrative (in one item, a group of naval gunners contract diarrhoea from spoiled meat; a few paragraphs later, there is a correction – it was the heat, not the meat). However, a couple of running themes emerge, which may or may not represent Fénéon's personal interests: it remains unclear whether he was under editorial guidance on the selection of items. The first concerns the regular theft, throughout the country, of telegraph and telephone wires. Time after time, vast lengths are snipped and silently removed. The culprits are rarely apprehended, until, close to the end of his stint, Fénéon is able to report:

> People were beginning to think the telegraph-cable thieves were supernatural. And yet one has been caught: Eugène Matifos, of Boulogne.

The second near-theme is the continuing battle between Church and State over the display of crucifixes and other religious paraphernalia in schools. A mayor is relieved of his duties 'on account of his zeal at keeping Jesus in the schools'; others 'for having put God back into schools or having prevented his being removed'; 'once again, Christ is on the walls . . .'; four more mayors are suspended for wanting 'to keep the spectacle of the death of God in the sight of school-children'; others want to 'restore to classroom walls the image of divine torture'. The sequence finds a comic narrative conclusion in:

> This time the crucifix is solidly bolted to the wall at Bouillé. So much for the prefect of Maine-et-Loire.

As can be seen, elegant variation is one of Fénéon's favourite techniques. What new way can be found of describing the latest violent yet sadly repetitive crime? One victim is 'mutilated in a way that specified the passionate nature of the crime'; another in a fashion that is 'permanently cancelling his virility'. A father kills his sexually active daughter for being 'insufficiently austere'; a day labourer admits that 'he often substituted for his wife his daughter Valentine, 14, who was 8 when the practice began'. Félicie de Doncker, an abortionist, is 'proficient at quelling the birth rate in Brabant'. Rustic rapists are cast as 'fauns', as in:

> Mme Olympe Fraisse relates that in the woods of Bordezac, Gard, a faun subjected her 66 years to prodigious abuses.

Or:

> M. Pierre de Condé was arrested at Craches for rape. Alcide Lenoux, who was also implicated, fled. The two fauns are 16 and 18.

Elegant variation shades into ironical euphemism, which shades into dandiacal detachment. Flaubert, in despair at the Franco-Prussian War, and trying to maintain the primacy of art, commented that in the long run, perhaps the only function of such carnage was to provide writers with a few fine scenes. So here, the function of the octogenarian Breton woman who hangs herself, or the 75-year-old man who dies of a stroke on the bowling lawn ('While his ball was still rolling he was no more'), or the 70-year-old who drops dead of sunstroke ('Quickly, his dog Fido ate his head') is to provide a sophisticated Parisian with a witty paragraph. As an aesthete-anarchist, Fénéon had always cultivated a detached gaiety of tone: a bomb became a 'delightful kettle' and the manner in which it killed six people showed 'intimate charm' (we are not far from Stockhausen's quickly retracted description of the World Trade Center attacks as 'the greatest artwork ever made'). So with the *Nouvelles*: are they a modernist's evocation of a harsh and absurd world, a subtle continuation of propaganda by word; or are they simply a classier expression of the press's traditional heartless sensationalism? Though they could, of course, be both.

Clive James once cruelly rebuked an *Observer* subeditor who had sought to sharpen his prose style and improve his jokes with the remark, 'Listen, if I wrote like that I'd be *you*.' Félix Fénéon might be the perfect counter-example: the sub who wrote better than the newspaper's main contributors. He knew how to shape a sentence, how to make three lines breathe, delay a key piece of information, introduce a quirky adjective, hold the necessary verb until last. Just fitting in the requisite facts is a professional skill; giving the whole item form, elegance, wit and surprise is an art.

But how much of an art, and of what resonance? The Futurists, despite Apollinaire's suggestion, didn't acknowledge Fénéon's model, quite possibly because they were utterly unaware of it. Sante quotes what they meant by *parole in libertà*: 'Literature having up to now glorified thoughtful immobility, ecstasy and slumber, we wish to exalt the aggressive moment, the feverish insomnia, the running, the perilous leap, the cuff and the blow.' That there was a great deal of daft windbaggery about the Futurists, this quote confirms; that Marinetti's words are proof of a 'common essence' with Fénéon's *nouvelles*, as Sante claims, strikes me as fantastical. So does the notion that they are 'a proto-Surrealist art form'.

Posterity likes to see itself predicted; modernism needs modernists *avant la lettre* even if the facts have to be fitted. Fénéon helped establish neo-Impressionism, and was the first owner of Seurat's *Bathing at Asnières* (when a dealer offered him a large sum for it, he replied, 'But what could I do with all that money, except buy it back from you?'); he supported Matisse and bought a Braque. But he was also the art critic who, when Apollinaire took him to see *Les Demoiselles d'Avignon* at the Bateau-Lavoir in 1907, turned to Picasso and said, 'You should stick to caricature.'

We could, if feeling theoretical, see the *Nouvelles* in terms of the literary crises Sartre described. Flaubert, with whom it all began, found the story of *Madame Bovary* in a provincial *faits divers.* Whether there was an actual cutting or not is beside the point; but as Fénéon might have put it:

> Delphine Delamare, 27, wife of a medical officer in Ry, displayed insufficient austerity. Worse, she ran up debts. To avoid paying them, she took poison.

From there, the nineteenth-century novel expanded and progressed, until there was nowhere left for it to go, so it folded itself back into the form it had come from, the *nouvelles en trois lignes*, waiting for the opportunity to unpack itself again. That might be one reading, and the fact that when fiction recovered its vitality it acknowledged no more debt to Fénéon than the Futurists did was appropriate: the 'invisible' writer had 'invisible' influence.

Or we could say that Fénéon, highly intelligent and ironical, found himself at a certain point in his life set to a task of journalistic drudgery. Over the long evenings at his desk at *Le Matin*, he made things as much fun for himself and his readers as was compatible with the needs of the slot. He took a long-established form and tweaked it, adding a personal stylistic touch while acknowledging that the nineteenth-century fundamentals of narrative and fact-conveying had to be respected. The *nouvelles* are the literary equivalent of the cocktail olive, and Fénéon should be remembered, and admired, for having devised a piquant new stuffing.

MICHEL HOUELLEBECQ AND
THE SIN OF DESPAIR

<hr />

I N 1998 I was one of the judges for the Prix Novembre in Paris: a prize given, as its month implies, late in the literary season. After the Goncourt had got it wrong, and after the stumblebum efforts by other prizes to correct Goncourt's errors, the Prix Novembre would issue its final, authoritative verdict on the year. It was unusual for a French prize in having a (slowly) rotating jury, foreign judges – Mario Vargas Llosa was also there – and serious money attached: about $30,000 to the winner.

That year the major prizes had all failed to honour Michel Houellebecq's *Les Particules élémentaires,* and for months *le cas Houellebecq* had been simmering. Schoolteachers had protested at the book's explicit sexuality; the author had been expelled from his own literary-philosophical group for intellectual heresy. Nor was it just the book that provoked; the guy himself did too. One female member of our jury declared that she had admired the novel until she watched its author on television. The Maecenas of the prize, a businessman whose interventions the previous year had been very low-key, made a lengthy and impassioned attack on Houellebecq. He seemed, at the very least, to be indicating where he didn't want his money to go.

In the course of a rather tense discussion, it was Vargas Llosa who came up with the best description of *Les Particules élémentaires*: 'insolent'. He meant it, naturally, as a term of praise.

There are certain books – sardonic and acutely pessimistic – which systematically affront all our current habits of living, and treat our presumptions of mind as the delusions of the cretinous. Voltaire's *Candide* might be taken as the perfect example of literary insolence. In a different way, La Roche-foucauld is deeply insolent; so is Beckett, bleakly, and Roth, exuberantly. The book of insolence finds its targets in such concepts as a purposeful God, a benevolent and orderly universe, human altruism, the existence of free will.

Houellebecq's novel – his second – was very French in its mixture of intellectuality and eroticism; it was reminiscent of Tournier in the evident pride it took in its own theoretical bone structure. It also had its faults: a certain heavy-handedness, and a tendency for the characters to make speeches rather than utter dialogue. But in its high ambition and intransigence, it was clearly superior to the other immediate contender for the prize, a novel which was very French in a different way: elegant, controlled and old-fashioned – or, rather, '*classique*', as I learned to say in judges' jargon.

Houellebecq squeaked it by a single vote. Afterwards I was talking to the president of the jury, writer and journalist Daniel Schneidermann, about the fuss our winner had kicked up in the press and on television. Perhaps, I suggested, it was just that he wasn't *médiatique* – mediagenic. 'On the contrary,' replied Schneidermann (who had voted for Houellebecq), 'he's *médiatique* by being *anti-médiatique*. It's very clever.' An hour or so later, in a gilded salon of the Hotel Bristol, before literary Paris's smartest, a shabby figure in a baggy sweater and rumpled scarlet jeans took his cheque and – in the spirit of his novel – declined to wallow in bourgeois expressions of pleasure or gratitude. Not all were charmed. 'It's an insult to the members of the jury', one French publisher whispered to me, 'for him to accept the prize without having washed or gone to the dry-cleaner's.'

Our Maecenas also got huffy, and announced the following

year that the Prix Novembre would be suspended for twelve months, so that we could discuss its future direction. Most jury members thought that this was unnecessary, not to say insolent; we decamped to a new sponsor and renamed ourselves the Prix Décembre. Meanwhile, the novel was translated into English as *Atomised*, and anglophones became aware of what Schneidermann had told me: its author was *médiatique* by being *anti-médiatique*. The literary world is one of the easiest in which to acquire a bad-boy reputation; and Houellebecq duly obliged. When the (female) profiler from the *Observer* visited him, he got catatonically drunk, collapsed face down into his dinner, and told her he'd only answer further questions if she slept with him. Houellebecq's wife was also enlisted, posing for the photographer in her underwear and offering a loyal quote of treasurable quality. 'Michel's not depressed,' she told the interviewer. 'It's the world that's depressing.'

If Houellebecq is, on the evidence of *Atomised*, the most potentially weighty French novelist to emerge since Tournier (and the wait has been long, and therefore overpraise understandable), his third novel, *Platform*, opens with a nod in an earlier direction. No French writer would begin a novel 'Father died last year' without specifically invoking Camus' *The Outsider*. Houellebecq's narrator is called Renault, perhaps hinting that such a man has become a mere cog in a mechanised society; but the name also chimes with Meursault, Camus' narrator. And for a clincher: Renault's father has been sleeping with his North African cleaner, Aïcha, whose brother beats the old man to death. When the son is brought face to face with his father's murderer, he reflects: 'If I had a gun, I would have shot without a second thought. Killing that little shit . . . seemed to me a morally neutral act.' Cut to Meursault's gunning-down of the Arab on the beach in Algiers, and to his similar moral indifference to the act.

But in the sixty years that lie between *The Outsider* and *Platform*, alienation and anomie have moved on. So have expressions of disrespect for the parent. As a schoolboy in the 1960s, I found Meursault's transgressive opening words – 'Mother died today. Or perhaps yesterday, I don't know' – registering like a slap (and I wasn't a pious son either). Nowadays, you have to slap harder:

> As I stood before the old man's coffin, unpleasant thoughts came to me. He had made the most out of life, the old bastard; he was a clever cunt. 'You had kids, you fucker,' I said spiritedly, 'you shoved your fat cock into my mother's cunt.' Well, I was a bit tense, I have to admit; it's not every day you have a death in the family.

Houellebecq ups the ante; but it's also his trademark to follow the coffinside vituperation with the wry 'Well, I was a bit tense'. *Atomised* was hard to summarise (it's about the third 'metaphysical mutation' of the last two thousand years, that of molecular biology, which will see cloning put an end to the fear of death and the miseries of genetic individualism . . .) without making it sound heavy; on the page, there was a satirical glee to its denunciations, drollery in the dystopia.

Platform begins very much in the mode of *Atomised*, with a radically detached male narrator, a child of the information age, excoriating the falseness of the world. He boasts the 'disinterested attitude appropriate to an accounts manager' towards almost everything. He is emotionally mute; socially too, and thus barely able to converse with Aïcha. When she begins criticising Islam, he more or less agrees, though he isn't entirely hard-line about it: 'Intellectually, I could manage to feel a certain attraction to Muslim vaginas.'

Anyone not yet offended? But Houellebecq, or rather 'Michel' as his narrator is elidingly called, has barely started. Snorting contempt is coming the way of the following: Frederick Forsyth and John Grisham; Jacques Chirac; the

Guide du Routard (a French equivalent of the Rough Guides); package tourists; France ('a sinister country, utterly sinister and bureaucratic'); the Chinese; the 'bunch of morons' who 'died for the sake of democracy' on Omaha Beach; most men; most women; children; the unattractive; the old; the West; Muslims; the French channel TV5; Muslims again; most artists; Muslims yet again; and finally, frequently, the narrator himself.

What does Michel approve of? Peep shows, massage parlours, pornography, Thai prostitutes, alcohol, Viagra (which helps you overcome the effects of the alcohol), cigarettes, non-white women, masturbation, lesbianism, troilism, Agatha Christie, double penetration, fellatio, sex tourism and women's underwear. You might have spotted an odd one out there. Frederick Forsyth may be a 'halfwit', while John Grisham's books are only good for wanking into: 'I ejaculated between two pages with a groan of satisfaction. They were going to stick together; didn't matter, it wasn't the kind of book you read twice.' But Agatha Christie receives two pages of adulation, mainly for her novel *The Hollow*, in which she makes clear that she understands the 'sin of despair'. This is the 'sin of cutting yourself off from all warm and living human contacts'; which is, of course, the sin of Michel. 'It is in our relations with other people', he remarks, 'that we gain a sense of ourselves; it's that, pretty much, that makes relations with other people unbearable.' Further: 'Giving up on life is the easiest thing to do'; and 'Anything can happen in life, especially nothing.'

The sin of despair is compounded when the sufferer is a hedonist. *Platform* is largely concerned with tourism, sex and the combination of the two. Tourism is currently the biggest single industry on the planet, a pure locus of supply and deliberately massaged demand. One key appeal for the novelist is tourism's psychology: not least the central, Flaubertian irony whereby anticipation and remembrance (the brochure's false promise of happiness, the holiday snap's grinning lie) often prove more vivid and reliable than the moment itself. One key danger for the novelist – not always avoided here – is that of easy satire: tourists make soft targets not just for terrorists.

Houellebecq sends Michel off on a sun-and-sex vacation; his largely crass companions include the acceptable, indeed positively attractive, Valérie, who works for the travel company. Much of the immediate plot turns on her attempts and those of her colleague Jean-Yves to revive an ailing branch of the corporation they work for. This is all adequately done, though Houellebecq's strengths and interests as a writer are not particularly those of traditional narrative. His approach to a scene, and a theme, often remind me of a joke long current in Euro circles. A British delegate to some EU committee outlines his country's proposals, which, being British, are typically pragmatic, sensible and detailed. The French delegate reflects noddingly on them for a considerable period of time, before delivering judgement: 'Well, I can see the plan will work in practice, but will it work in theory?'

Thus the primary, obvious link between sex and tourism is the carnal, interpersonal (and impersonal) one. But just as important for Houellebecq is to find the theoretical connection. Which he does: both sex and tourism exemplify the free market at its most free. Sex has always appeared capitalistic to Houellebecq. Here is his formulation from his first novel, *Whatever*:

> In an economic system where unfair dismissal is prohibited, every person more or less manages to find their place. In a sexual system where adultery is prohibited, every person more or less manages to find a bed mate. In a totally liberal economic system certain people accumulate considerable fortunes; others stagnate in unemployment and misery. In a totally liberal sexual system certain people have a varied and exciting

erotic life; others are reduced to masturbation and solitude.

This kind of swift, audacious linkage is Houellebecq at his best; he loves nothing more than working over what in *Atomised* he called 'the North American libidinal-hedonist option'. But his actual writing about sex, in *Platform*, is curiously both pornographic and sentimental. Pornographic in the sense of taking all its moves and images from pornography; who put what where and moved it whither until a convulsive spurt-'n'-groan; also, written like pornography of a decent, middle-ranking kind. Sentimental in that the novel's really nice, straightforward characters are Oriental masseuses and prostitutes, who are presented without flaws, diseases, pimps, addictions or hang-ups. Pornographic *and* sentimental in that nothing ever goes wrong with the sexual act: pneumatic bliss is always obtained, no one ever says No or Stop or even Wait, and you just have to beckon at a non-white-skinned maid on the hotel terrace for her to pop into the room, quickly reveal she is braless, and slide seamlessly into a threesome. Houellebecq sees through everything in the world except commercial sex, which he describes – perhaps appropriately – like one who believes every word and picture of a holiday brochure.

And then there is love. 'I really love women,' Michel tells us on the opening page. Later, he elaborates: 'My enthusiasm for pussy' is one of 'my few remaining recognisable, fully human qualities'. Despite 'loving women', Michel pointedly never refers to his mother. And when this depressed, old-at-forty sex tourist gradually finds himself becoming involved with Valérie, you wonder how Houellebecq will handle it. After all, it is a piece of literary insolence to make such a character fall in love in the first place. So how is love different for Michel from commercial sex? Happily, not too much. Valérie, though at first appearing rather dowdy and browbeaten, turns out to have wonderful breasts; she is also as good in bed as Thai prostitutes; and she doesn't just go along with three-somes, she instigates them. She is by nature docile; yet she holds down a good job and is very well paid; like him she scorns designer clothes. And that's about it, really. They don't do any of that old stuff like talking about feelings, or thinking about them; they don't go out much together, though he does take her to a wife-swap bar and an S & M club. He does a spot of cooking; she is often so tired from work that it isn't until the next morning that she can give him a blow job. This is not so much insolent as fictionally disappointing. Oh, and Valérie has to die, of course, just when she has found happiness and the couple have decided to live on a paradise island. The set-up, and execution, of this would have been improved upon by Grisham or Forsyth.

Why, to go back to the start, does Michel hate his father so? This is one question a normally inquisitive reader might ask after that coffinside denunciation. What do we learn of this 'old bastard', this 'clever cunt', this 'moron in shorts', this 'hideously representative element' of the twentieth century? That he was seventy when he died, that Aïcha was 'very fond' of him, that he exercised a lot and owned a Toyota Land Cruiser. Hardly grounds enough, you might think. But we also learn, further on, that this monster had once been struck down by a sudden, inexplicable depression. 'His mountain-eering friends stood around awkwardly, powerless in the face of the disease. The reason he played so much sport, he once told me, was to stupefy himself, to stop himself thinking.' This is all new (we hadn't been told before that the father was a mountaineer); and you might think, since Michel is himself depressed, that it might have been grounds for sympathy. But this is all we get, and the father swiftly disappears from the narrative, as he does from Michel's thoughts.

Within the novel, the filial hatred is just an inexplicable given. However, book chat (not always to be despised) turns up an interview Houellebecq gave to *Lire* magazine a few years ago. The novelist's parents abandoned him when he was five, leaving him in the care of a grandmother. 'My father', says Houellebecq, 'developed early on a sense of excessive guilt. He once told me the strangest thing: that he devoted himself to intense physical activity so much because it stopped him thinking. He was a mountain guide.'

No reason why this strange confession shouldn't be used by a fiction writer; but if it is to work, it needs to be supported fictionally. In *Platform* the slippage between 'Michel R' and Michel H is more serious than this little bit of autobiographical leaching might suggest. There are problems with the narrative, officially a first-person account by Michel R, but one which dodges into the third person if it needs to tell us what only Michel H can know. (There is even an incompetent moment when Michel R gives us his judgement on a character he hasn't yet met.) Within Michel himself, there is also some curious slippage. Thus he sets off on holiday with 'two American best-sellers that I'd bought pretty much at random at the airport' (this despite feeling *de haut en bas* about Forsyth and Grisham); he also has the *Guide du Routard*. Fair enough for a sex tourist, you might think. Later, a bit surprisingly, he panics at the thought of having nothing to read. Later still, when back home, he turns out to be an assiduous reader of Auguste Comte and Milan Kundera; he also quotes confidently from Kant, Schopenhauer and social theoreticians. Is this credibly the same character, or someone shifting to meet the needs of the moment?

This sense of Houellebecq being a clever man who is a less than clever novelist obtrudes most in the novel's dealings with Islam. Structurally, the function of what Michel calls 'the absurd religion' appears to be to deliver, at the end, an extreme and murderous disapproval of the happy sex tourists. Its running presence, however, consists in a trio of outbursts. First from Aïcha, who launches unasked into a denunciation of her Mecca-stupefied father and her useless brothers: 'They get blind drunk on pastis and all the while they strut around like the guardians of the one true faith, and they treat me like a slut because I prefer to go out and work rather than marry some stupid bastard like them.' Next there is the Egyptian once encountered by Michel in the Valley of the Kings, an immensely cultivated and intelligent genetic engineer, for whom Muslims are 'the losers of the Sahara' and Islam a religion born among 'filthy Bedouins' who did nothing but 'bugger their camels'. Then there is the Jordanian banker met in Bangkok, who in the course of general denunciation points out that the sexual paradise promised to Islamic martyrs is much more cheaply obtainable in any hotel massage parlour. Extraordinary that three casual meetings on three different continents should turn up three vociferous Arab Islam-despisers who disappear from the narrative immediately after their work is done. This isn't so much an author with his thumb on the scales as one clambering into the weighing pan and doing a tap dance. (Book-chat parenthesis: Houellebecq told *Lire* magazine that his mother had become a Muslim, adding, 'I can't bear Islam.')

Before I started reading this novel, a French friend gave me an unexpected warning: 'There's a scene where the narrator and his girlfriend and another woman have a threesome in the hammam at the thalassotherapy centre in Dinard. Well, I've been there,' he went on, his tone hardening, 'and it's *just not possible*.' He is not a pedantic man, and his attitude surprised me. But now I quite understand it. Fictional insolence is a high-risk venture: it must, as *Atomised* did, take you by the ear and brain and frog-march you, convince you with the force of its rhetoric and the rigour of its despair. It should allow no time for reactions like, Hang on, that's not true; or, Surely people aren't that bad; or even, Actually, I'd like to think this one over. *Platform*, fuelled more by opinions and riffs and moments of provocation than by thorough narrative, allows such questionings to enter the reader's head far too often. Is sex like this? Is love like this? Are Muslims like this? Is humanity like this? Is Michel depressed, or is the world depressing? Camus, who began by creating in Meursault one of the most disaffected characters in post-war fiction, ended by writing *The First Man*, in which ordinary lives are depicted with the richest observation and sympathy. It seems less likely that Houellebecq will ever succeed in purging the sin of despair.

TRANSLATING *MADAME BOVARY*

I F YOU GO to the web page of the restaurant L'Huîtrière (3 rue des Chats Bossus, Lille) and click on 'translate', the zealous automaton you have stirred up will instantly render everything into English, including the address. And it comes out as '3 street cats humped'. Translation is clearly too important a task to be left to machines. But what sort of human should it be given to?

Imagine that you are about to read a great French novel for the first time, and can only do so in your native English. The book itself is over 150 years old. What would – should – do – you want? The impossible, of course. But what sort of impossible? For a start, you would probably want it not to read like 'a translation'. You want it to read as if it had originally been written in English – even if, necessarily, by an author deeply knowledgeable about France. You would want it not to clank and whirr as it dutifully renders every single nuance, turning the text into an exposition of the novel rather than the novel itself. You would want it to provoke in you most of the same reactions as it would provoke in a French reader (though you would want some sense of distance, and the pleasure of exploring a different world). But what sort of French reader? One from the late 1850s, or the early 2010s? Would you want the novel to have its original effect, or an effect coloured by the later history of French fiction, including the consequences of this very novel's existence? Ideally, you would want to understand every period reference – for instance, to Trafalgar pudding, or Ignorantine friars, or *Mathieu Laensberg*

– without needing to flick downwards or onwards to footnotes. Finally, if you want the book in 'English', what sort of English do you choose? Put simply, on the novel's first page, do you want the schoolboy Charles Bovary's trousers to be held up by braces, or do you want his pants to be held up by suspenders? The decisions, and the coloration, are irrevocable.

So we might fantasise the translator of our dreams: someone, naturally, who admires the novel and its author, and who sympathises with its heroine; a woman, perhaps, to help us better navigate the sexual politics of the time; someone with excellent French and better English, perhaps with a little experience of translating in the opposite direction as well. Then we make a key decision: should this translator be ancient or modern? Flaubert's contemporary, or ours? After a little thought, we might plump for an Englishwoman of Flaubert's time, whose prose would inevitably be free of anachronism or other style-jarringness. And if she was of the time, then might we not reasonably imagine the author helping her? Let's push it further: the translator not only knows the author, but lives in his house, able to observe his spoken as well as his written French. They might work side by side on the text for as long as it takes. And now let's push it to the limit: the female English translator might become the Frenchman's lover – they always say that the best way to learn a language is through pillow talk.

As it happens, this dream was once a reality. The first known translation of *Madame Bovary* was undertaken from a fair copy of the manuscript by Juliet Herbert, governess to Flaubert's niece Caroline, in 1856–7. Quite possibly, she was Gustave's lover; certainly, she gave him English lessons. 'In six months, I will read Shakespeare like an open book,' he boasted; and together they translated Byron's 'Prisoner of Chillon' into French. (Back in 1844, Flaubert claimed to his friend Louis de Cormenin that he had translated *Candide* into English.) In May 1857, Flaubert wrote to Michel Lévy, the Parisian publisher of *Madame Bovary*, that 'An English translation which *fully* satisfies me is being made under my eyes. If one is going to appear in England, I want it to be this one and not any other one.' Five years later, he was to call Juliet Herbert's work 'a masterpiece'. But by this time it – and she – were beginning to disappear from literary history. Though Flaubert had asked Lévy to fix Juliet up with an English publisher, and believed he had written to Richard Bentley & Sons about the matter, no such letter from Paris survives in the Bentley archives (perhaps because Lévy secretly objected to the idea and declined to act on it). The manuscript was lost, and so – more or less – was Juliet Herbert, until her resurrection in 1980 by Hermia Oliver's *Flaubert and an English Governess*.

So the British reader had to wait another three decades – until 1886, six years after the author's death – for the first published translation of *Madame Bovary*. It too was made by a woman, Eleanor Marx-Aveling (Marx's daughter – a quiet irony, given Flaubert's caustic views on the Commune), as is the very latest, by the American short-story writer – and Proust translator – Lydia Davis. In between, most of the nineteen or so versions have been made by men. The best-known of them are Francis Steegmuller and Gerard Hopkins; and though Steegmuller did write some fiction – including mysteries under the name of David Keith – it's a fair bet that Davis is the best fiction writer ever to translate the novel. Which suggests a further question to the opening list: would you rather have your great novel translated by a good writer or a less good one? This is not as idle a question as it seems. That perfect translator must be a writer able to subsume him- or herself into the greater writer's text and identity. Writer-translators with their own style and world view might become fretful at the necessary self-abnegation; on the other hand, disguising oneself as another writer is an act of the imagin-ation, and perhaps easier for the better writer. So if Rick Moody tells us that Lydia Davis is 'the best prose stylist in

America', and Jonathan Franzen that 'Few writers now working make the words on the page matter more', does this make her better or worse equipped to render the best prose stylist of nineteenth-century France into twenty-first-century American English? Davis's stories, typically from two or three lines to two or three pages, are decidedly un-Flaubertian in scope and extent; they vary from the wry episode and rapt reverie to the slightly arch two-liner; and if there is French influence around it is from a later date (thus Davis's 'The Race of the Patient Motorcyclists' seems to owe a debt to Jarry). Her own life is clearly the basis for some of the stories, whereas Flaubert's aesthetic was famously based on self-exclusion. On the other hand, Davis's work shares the Flaubertian virtues of compression, irony and an extreme sense of control. And if Flaubert in his monasticism and exemplary pertinacity is a writer's writer, Davis was described to me recently by an American novelist as a 'writer's writer's writer'. That her translation of *Madame Bovary* was deemed worthy of serialisation by *Playboy* magazine – which puffed it as 'The most scandalous novel of all time' on the cover – is a noisier irony of which Flaubert might well have approved. The publicity sheet for the Viking (US) edition calls Emma 'the original desperate housewife', which, cheesy though it sounds, isn't far off the mark. *Madame Bovary* is many things – a perfect piece of fictional machinery, the pinnacle of realism, the slaughterer of Romanticism, a complex study of failure – but it is also the first great shopping-and-fucking novel.

At least none of those nineteen or so translators has needed to recast its title; problems start, rather, with the subtitle, '*Moeurs de province*'. You can have 'Provincial Manners' (Marx-Aveling), 'Life in a Country Town' (Hopkins, 1948), 'A Tale of Provincial Life' (Alan Russell, 1950), 'Provincial Lives' (Geoffrey Wall, 1992), or 'Provincial Ways' (Lydia Davis). No one, as far as I can see, has adopted the cousinly subtitle of *Middlemarch*: 'A Study of Provincial Life'. Several versions – including, rather surprisingly, that of Francis Steegmuller (1957) – simply delete it. Subtitles can seem fussy and old-fashioned (thus the current Penguin *Middlemarch* dispenses with Eliot's five subsidiary words), but omission seems a little perverse. Many translators (or publishers) also omit the next words in the novel – the dedication to Maître Sénard, who got Flaubert off the charge of outraging morality and religion when the novel, still in serial form, was prosecuted. Lydia Davis, an impressive completist, includes both this and the other, and more important, dedicatory page of the first edition, to Flaubert's partner-in-literature Louis Bouilhet. Though even here the translator enters a world of micro-pedantry, because there is a choice of order: authenticity might favour the first edition, which begins with the Bouilhet dedication (in fact, a printer's misleaving), while sense will prefer the corrected edition of 1873, which opens with the Sénard tribute.

But then translation involves micro-pedantry as much as the full yet controlled use of the linguistic imagination. The plainest sentence is full of hazard; often the choices available seem to be between different percentages of loss. It's no surprise that Lydia Davis took three years to translate *Madame Bovary* – some translations need as long as the book itself took to write, a few even longer. John Rutherford's magisterial version of Leopoldo Alas's *La Regenta* – a kind of Spanish *Bovary* – used up, according to his calculation, five times as much of his life as it had of the original author's. 'Translation is a strange business,' he noted in his introduction, 'which sensible people no doubt avoid.' Take a simple detail from the first pages of Flaubert's novel. In his early years, Charles Bovary is allowed by his parents to run wild. He follows the ploughmen, throwing clods of earth at the crows; he minds turkeys and does a little bell-ringing. Flaubert awards such activities a paragraph, and then summarises the consequences of this pre-adolescent life in two short sentences which he pointedly sets out as a separate paragraph:

*Aussi poussa-t-il comme un chêne. Il acquit de fortes mains,
de belles couleurs.*

The meaning is quite clear; there are no hidden traps or false
friends. If you want to try putting this into English yourself
first, then look away now. Here are six attempts from the last
125 years to translate yet not traduce:

1) Meanwhile he grew like an oak; he was strong
   of hand, fresh of colour.
2) And so he grew like an oak-tree, and acquired a
   strong pair of hands and a fresh colour.
3) He grew like a young oak-tree. He acquired
   strong hands and a good colour.
4) He throve like an oak. His hands grew strong
   and his complexion ruddy.
5) And so he grew up like an oak. He had strong
   hands, a good colour.
6) And so he grew like an oak. He acquired strong
   hands, good colour.

All contain the same information, but only the words 'he',
'like' and 'strong' are consistent to all six. Some of the matters
these translators would have considered (on a scale from
pertinent reflection to gut feel) would include:

- Whether to lay the paragraph out as two
  sentences or one; if the latter, then whether the
  break should be marked by a comma or a
  semicolon.
- Whether, indeed, to lay it out as a separate
  paragraph anyway: thus 1) chooses to run it on
  at the end of the previous paragraph, which
  makes its summarising effect less pointed.
- Whether *pousser* implies more vigour than the

English 'grow': hence 4)'s 'throve' and 5)'s addition of the intensifying 'up'.

- Whether *acquit* is best rendered by a neutral word like 'had' or 'was'; or whether it is a verb indicating a kind of action, intended to parallel *poussa*. Hence 'acquired' or 'grew' – though if you have 'grew' here, you need a different verb in the first sentence: hence 'throve'.

- Whether you need to – or can – keep the balance of *de fortes mains, de belles couleurs*. Only 1) does this by putting them both in the singular; the rest introduce an imbalance of number.

- What to do about *belles couleurs*. All six translators agree that there is no way of preserving the plural form. But a) do you need to unpack this a little, and indicate that the young lad is acquiring a 'fresh' or 'ruddy' colour, or indeed 'complexion' (which decides that *couleurs* is limited to the face – though reference has already been made, on the novel's first page, to his 'red wrists'); or b) is it self-evident where the lad is, and what is happening to his skin, so a non-specific 'good' echoes a non-specific *belles*?

All these six versions – given in chronological order – have their virtues; none is obviously superior. 1) is Marx-Aveling, a version which, as Davis notes in her introduction, caused Nabokov 'much indignation in his marginal notations but to which he resorted in teaching the novel'; 2) is Russell; 3) Hopkins; 4), which even on this short evidence looks freer than the others, is Steegmuller; 5) is Wall; and 6) Davis. Wall and Davis are the two who stick closest to the original sentence structure and are least 'interpretative'.

There is a slightly pretentious term in wine tasting and

wine writing called 'mouthfeel'. (It is also slightly baffling – where else might you feel wine if not in your mouth? On your foot?) The *Oxford Companion to Wine* calls it a 'non-specific tasting term, used particularly for red wines, to indicate those textural attributes, such as smoothness, that produce tactile sensations on the surface of the oral cavity'. There is similar mouthfeel about translation. The general trend of translation over the last century and more has been away from smoothness and towards authenticity, away from a reorganising interpretativeness which aims for the flow of English prose, towards a close-reading fidelity – enjoy those tannins! – which seeks to echo the original language. We no longer use the verb 'to English' – it sounds proprietorial, even imperialist – but when Flaubert was first being translated it was still in use: thus the first London and New York edition of *Salammbô* – published in 1886, the same year as Marx-Aveling's *Madame Bovary* – is described on its title page as having been 'Englished' by (wait for it) 'M. French Sheldon'. This progress away from 'Englishing' can be seen in the six versions of Charles's growing (up) quoted above. Similarly, in Chekhov translation, Constance Garnett has been succeeded by Ronald Hingley. Succeeded, and yet not supplanted: some of us continue to read the Garnett translations. Mainly because they do the time-travelling work instantly, and give a better illusion of being a reader back then, rather than a reader now inspecting a text from long ago through precision optical instruments. It may be, however, that something different, or additional, is going on: a kind of imprinting. The first translation we read of a classic novel, like the first recording we hear of a piece of classical music, 'is' and remains that novel, that symphony. Subsequent interpreters may have a better grasp of the language, or play the piece on period instruments, but that initial version always takes some shifting.

The authentic rendering of every last nuance of meaning cannot be the sole purpose of translation. Because if it becomes so, then it leads to the act of eccentric defiance that is Nabokov's *Eugene Onegin*. In his 1955 poem 'On Translating *Eugene Onegin*', Nabokov, addressing Pushkin, writes of turning 'Your stanza patterned on a sonnet, / Into my honest roadside prose – / All thorn, but cousin to your rose.' When Nabokov's version of the poem came out in 1964, it was prose laid out in stanza form, and more woody stalk than thorn. Readers of the poem in English are best advised to have the two volumes of Nabokov's headmasterly commentary to hand while apprehending the poem's dance and flow through, say, Charles Johnston's version. An even weirder example of fidelity leading to perversity is Dillwyn Knox's 1929 translation of Herodas for the Loeb Classical Library. Knox's brilliant niece Penelope Fitzgerald describes the outcome in *The Knox Brothers* with a kind of sympathetic glee:

> The language of the Mimes is precious, with unpleasant affected archaisms, and an honest translation, it seemed to Dilly, must be the same. Cloistered in his study . . . Dilly worked out his English equivalent to Herodas. 'La no reke hath she of what I say, but standeth goggling at me more agape than a crab' is a typical sentence, while 'Why can't you tell me what they cost?' comes out as 'Why mumblest ne freetongued descryest the price?' Satisfied, Dilly corrected the proofs; he read the reviews, all of which praised the accuracy of the text but considered the translation a complete failure, with indifference. 'If I am unintelligible,' he wrote, 'it is because Herodas was.'

Davis, in her introduction, notes that Gerard Hopkins's version has 'added material in almost every sentence'; while Steegmuller produced a 'nicely written, engaging version, smoother than Flaubert's, with regular restructuring of the sentences and judicious omissions and additions'. Does this

sound a trifle patronising to America's greatest Flaubertian?
Here is a typical addition (or rather, substitution) which will
act as a good test of the reader's reaction. When Léon goes
to meet Emma inside Rouen Cathedral, he first has to get
past a verger standing in the left-hand doorway beneath a
statue which Flaubert refers to as '*Marianne dansant*'. This was
the popular nickname for a carving of Salome dancing on
her hands before Herod. What do you do about this? Almost
all translators render it as 'Marianne Dancing' or 'The Dancing
Marianne'. If you leave these words unannotated, readers will
naturally imagine some cheery folkloric image. If you annotate
them, then you divert the reader away for a guidebook
moment – as elbow-tugging as the intrusive verger will prove
to be to Léon and Emma. (You can half solve it, as Davis
does, by having notes at the back but without indication in
the text of their existence; so readers may find the solution,
but perhaps not at the right time.) Or, as Steegmuller alone
does, in his unannotated version, you can cut to the chase
and write: 'The verger was just then standing in the left
doorway, under the figure of the dancing Salome.' This is
instantly comprehensible, and has the additional virtue of
pointing up this image of lasciviousness beneath which Léon
passes on his way to the tryst. (Inside the cathedral, this theme
is continued: when the verger reaches the tomb of the Comte
de Brézé, he solemnly points out Diane de Poitiers as a
grieving widow, while the rest of us know her as a king's
mistress – also, as Emma is soon to be, the lover of a younger
man.) Given that there is probably no one in Rouen who
still refers to the statue as '*Marianne dansant*', there is much
to be said for Steegmuller's solution. But some would find it
overly interventionist.

The root feature of Davis's translation is a close attention
to Flaubert's grammar and sentence structure, and an attempt
to mirror it in English. For instance, observance of the
'comma splice' – where two main clauses are connected by

a comma rather than an 'and' – or of subtle tense changes imperceptible to others (and sometimes imperceptible in English). In the earlier example (*Il acquit de fortes mains, de belles couleurs*), she writes 'the boy had good colour' where Wall has 'the boy had a good colour': dropping the article retains the original plain adjective–noun balance. In her introduction, Davis castigates some of her predecessors for wanting 'simply to tell this engrossing story in their own preferred manner'. Interviewed by *The Times*, she expanded on this: 'I've found that the ones that are written with some flair and some life to them are not all that close to the original; the ones that are more faithful may be kind of clunky.' This is the paradox and bind of translation. If to be 'faithful' is to be 'clunky', then it is also to be unfaithful, because Flaubert was not a 'clunky' writer. He moves between registers; he cuts into the lyric with the prosaic; but this is language whose every sentence, word, syllable has been tested aloud again and again. Flaubert said that a line of prose should be as rhythmical, sonorous and unchangeable as a line of poetry. He said that he aimed only at beauty, and wrote *Madame Bovary* because he hated realism (an exasperated, self-deluding claim, but still). He said that prose is like hair: it shines with combing. He combed all the time. As for those imprecise translators who nevertheless bring 'flair' and 'life' to the novel: where does that flair and life usually come from, if not the novel itself? Davis concludes: 'So what I'm trying to do is what I think hasn't been done, which is to create a well-written translation that's also very close, very faithful to the French.' This is a high claim; though I doubt any of those previous translators would have thought they were trying to do anything very different.

Davis's quest to be 'very close, very faithful' to the French works best when the Flaubertian sentence is plain and declaratory. Take that great moment of delinquent self-awareness: '*Emma retrouvait dans l'adultère toutes les platitudes du mariage.*'

Davis's 'Emma was rediscovering in adultery all the platitudes of marriage' exactly reproduces the French, and has exactly the same effect. You might think hers is the obvious translation until you compare other versions. Both Steegmuller and Hopkins diminish the line by recasting it, and even Wall, who is closest to Davis, misses out the necessary, intensifying 'all'. On the other hand, a page or two later there is this equally key sentence: '*Tout et elle-même lui étaient insupportables.*' This is an unusual sentence. A usual sentence might be '*Tout lui était insupportable; elle-même comprise*' or '*y compris elle-même*'. Flaubert specifically links the *Tout et elle-même* and it is a mistake to decouple them, as Davis does, into 'Everything seemed unbearable to her, even herself' (which adds the clunk of a repeated 'her'). Wall also goes awry here: 'It was quite unbearable, beginning with herself.' Hopkins unpacks it perhaps too much: 'She hated everything and everyone, including herself.' Steegmuller is best, with: 'She loathed everything, including herself.' But even this doesn't convey the full effect of that simple *et* – which is to indicate a separation of self from the world which will culminate in the deed which finally does separate Emma's self from the world.

So Davis's division of previous translators into flair-bringers and clunkheads doesn't really hold; nor does her claim to offer the best of both worlds. Two further examples:

1) After Emma's seduction by Rodolphe, there is a paragraph describing her post-coital, semi-pantheistic experience of the nature surrounding her, and with which she is for the moment in harmony. But with the last sentence, Flaubert cuts this mood brutally: '*Rodolphe, le cigare aux dents, raccommodait avec son canif une des deux brides cassée.*' This great anti-romantic moment has Rodolphe turning both to another physical pleasure (as Gurov is to do with his watermelon in Chekhov's 'The Lady with the Little Dog'), and to masculine, practical matters. All the versions cited here begin, unsurprisingly, with 'Rodolphe, a cigar between his teeth . . .' Wall goes on:

> was mending one of the two broken reins with his little knife.

Steegmuller:

> was mending a broken bridle with his penknife.

Hopkins:

> was busy with his knife, mending a break in one of the bridles.

Davis:

> was mending with his penknife one of the bridles, which had broken.

Rein or bridle? Knife, little knife, or penknife? The difference is slight; all the versions contain the same information. Flaubert's sentence does its business by not drawing attention to itself; its very downbeatness is the point, after the more rhapsodic prose that has preceded it. Wall, Steegmuller and Hopkins all get this. Davis doesn't. Instead, she 'faithfully' sticks to Flaubert's sentence structure. But English grammar is not French grammar, and so the quiet '*cassée*' (which for all its quietness also hints at Rodolphe's 'breaking' of Emma) has to be unpacked into a 'which had broken' – a phrase which now seems pretty redundant, as what would he mend that wasn't broken? The sentence has a clunkiness which is imported, rather than faithfully transmitted, and quite un-Flaubertian.

  2) During Charles and Emma's visit to the opera in Rouen – that greatest of the three great antiphonally constructed scenes in the novel – Emma's inner emotional life, her hopes and memories, are played off against the extravagantly exteriorised emotions of *Lucia di Lammermoor*. As her thoughts and

feelings swirl, Emma at one point comes to recognise that both art and life are inadequate in their different ways. This is a key sentence in the novel: '*Elle connaissait à présent la petitesse des passions que l'art exagérait.*' It is a calm, balanced sentence, in three parts, with a triple alliteration, the part containing the second and third *p* making up the central phrase. The choice for *petitesse* lies normally between 'paltriness' and 'pettiness', neither of which is perfect, as they have a slightly more disapproving tinge than *petitesse*. Wall's version has the weight and progress of the original:

> For now she knew the pettiness of the passions that art exaggerates.

Hopkins takes the alliteration elsewhere:

> She knew now the triviality of those passions which art paints so much larger than life.

Steegmuller retains the triple alliteration:

> Now she well knew the true paltriness of the passions that art painted so large.

Davis has:

> She knew, now, how paltry were the passions exaggerated by art.

She needlessly turns the first major noun into an adjective, then reverses the grammar of the final phrase. But the main failing of the sentence is those first three words: 'knew, now, how' – both a wail of assonance and a stuttering of rhythm far from the original.

A translation can't be read before the period in which it

is written: this is both obvious, and a kind of brute annoyance. And it can't – or at least, shouldn't – be written in a pastiche of the original work's period. It must be written for the contemporary reader, yet give that reader the same, or a similar, ease or difficulty as an original reader would have had. And just as there can be delinquent looseness, so there can be misguided over-accuracy. It is very difficult to suggest (except in footnotes and introduction) the general literary context in which a book is written, which is central to the writer. Books are often written *against* – against romanticism, against authorial ego and intervention, against the notion that some themes are 'higher' than others. There is a linguistic context too: thus Michael Hofmann, introducing his translation of *Metamorphosis*, quotes Klaus Wagenbach to the effect that 'the characteristic purity of Kafka, the sober construction of his sentences and the paucity of his vocabulary are not understandable without his background in Prague German'. Further, no two languages' grammars match, and their vocabularies diverge (English having many more words and choices than French). Even punctuations have different weights: thus the English exclamation mark is shoutier than the French, so some of Flaubert's have to be excised; Wall cuts more than Davis, who, at times, adds extra ones. Nor do languages develop over time at the same rate. So, in the case of *Madame Bovary*, you are having to juggle the French writer then, the French reader then and now, the English translator now, the English reader then and now.

Nowadays, at least, books are generally translated with less of a time lag (*La Regenta* was first published in 1884–5, and not rendered into English until 1984). Translators can quiz writers about what they mean, by email, or even in person: Don Delillo had a London conference for his European translators of *Underworld*, whose problems began as the novel does: with a sixty-page baseball game. But translation is not always, or necessarily, about managing loss. When my novel *Flaubert's Parrot* was being translated into German, my editor in Zurich modestly suggested some additional flourishes: for instance, a pun on Flaubert as a 'flea-bear', and a German slang phrase for masturbation which literally means 'to shake from the palm tree'. Since Flaubert, at this point of my novel, was being masturbated in Egypt, this felt like a happy improvement on the English text. Adding something extra for German readers seemed a kind of fair-trade translation. But this advantage encloses a new danger: that of the writer anticipating this amiable to-and-fro with translator or foreign editor. I remember hearing one British novelist admit in a radio interview that he had paused at one point in his writing, thought of the pain he might be inflicting on his Scandinavian translators, and decided to make things easier for them. Apart from this being a denial of your own language, it can easily lead to the sort of international prose that is like an airline meal: it feeds all, doesn't actually poison anyone, but isn't noticeably nutritious.

To compare several different versions of *Madame Bovary* is not to observe a process of accumulation, some gradual but inevitable progress towards certainty and authority (except in the occasional discarding of error); rather, it is to gaze at a sequence of approximations, a set of deliquescences. How could it be otherwise when almost every word of the French can be rendered in several different ways? Consider the moment when Emma, Charles and Léon are eating ice cream in a café by the harbour, having walked out before the final scene of *Lucia*. Charles naively suggests that his wife stay on in the city to catch the next performance – an action which is to precipitate her affair with Léon. Charles addresses his wife (the banality of phrase contrasting with the recent extravagances of Donizetti) as '*mon petit chat*'. Marx-Aveling has 'pussy', Mildred Marmur (1964) 'my kitten', Wall 'my pussy-cat', Hopkins 'darling', Steegmuller 'sweetheart', Russell and Davis 'my pet'. Marx-Aveling's endearment would work then but sadly not now; Marmur's is good; Wall's brings in the slightly unwanted flavour of a bad Dean Martin movie; Steegmuller and Hopkins deliberately duck the felinity (you could argue that the French is already drained of it anyway); while Russell and Davis, mixing banality and distant animality, have found the best solution. Probably. At least, for the moment. You can understand why Rutherford called translation a 'strange business' which 'sensible people' should best avoid.

Davis's *Madame Bovary* is a linguistically careful version, in the modern style, rendered into an unobtrusively American English. At its best, it conveys the precision – which some think dryness – of Flaubert's prose in this novel, while its syntactical mirroring of the French sometimes brings us closer to Flaubert. At its worst, it takes us too far away from English, and makes us less aware of Flaubert's prose than of Davis being aware of Flaubert's prose. And such defects may come from something ordinary but surprising: a lack of sufficient love for the work being translated. In her *Times* interview, Lydia Davis explained:

> I was asked to do the Flaubert, and it was hard to say no to another great book – so-called. I didn't actually like *Madame Bovary*. I find what he does with the language really interesting; but I wouldn't say that I warm to it as a book . . . And I like a heroine who thinks and feels . . . well, I don't find Emma Bovary admirable or likeable – but Flaubert didn't either. I do a lot of things that people don't think a translator does. They think: 'She loves *Madame Bovary*, she's read it three times in French, she's always wanted to translate it and she's urging publishers to do another translation, and she's done all the background reading . . .' but none of that is true.

Perhaps some of this is the translator's equivalent of being demob-happy – three years slogging across occupied France, it's no wonder she throws her cap in the air at having come out alive. Though what does Lydia Davis mean by saying that Emma Bovary doesn't 'think' or 'feel'? The novel is all about the perils of (wrong) thinking and (false, or unwisely directed) feeling. Perhaps she means 'doesn't think or feel in a way that I approve'. As for complaining that Emma isn't 'admirable or likeable' – this sounds like the most basic book-group objection. Davis's *Madame Bovary* shows that it's possible to produce a more than acceptable version of a book with which you are comparatively out of sympathy. In that sense, it confirms that translation requires an act of the imagination as well as a technician's proficiency. If you want a freer translation, Steegmuller is best; for a tighter one, go to Wall. And perhaps one day Juliet Herbert's lost 'masterpiece' will turn up, and we shall be able to compare it to its successors – and see a new way of necessarily falling short.

N OVELS CONSIST OF words, evenly and democratically spaced; though some may acquire higher social rank by italicisation or capitalisation. In most novels, this democracy spreads wider: every word is as important as every other word. In better novels, certain words have higher specific gravity than other words. This is something the better novelist does not draw attention to, but lets the better reader discover.

There are many ways of preparing to read a novel. You might prefer to approach it in proper and delighted ignorance. You might like to know a few basics about the author (Wharton, 1862–1937), her social origins (New York, old money), literary company (Henry James), land of exile (France), financial, marital and sexual status (rich, distressing, largely unfulfilled), and so on. You might want information inclining you to read the novel in as autobiographical way as it is possible to do (in which case, you will have to go elsewhere). You might, less prejudicingly, prefer to have simple facts of literary chronology and positioning: thus *The Reef* was published in 1912, seven years after Wharton had made her name with *The House of Mirth*, and is definingly placed between her grimmest novel, *Ethan Frome*, and her greatest novel of Franco-American interrelationship, *The Custom of the Country*. You might like such information decorated with literary gossip which warmingly defines the author: in the year she published *The Reef*, Wharton, having previously campaigned unsuccessfully to get Henry James the Nobel Prize, performed an act of literary generosity rare in any times and hard to imagine taking place today. She asked her publishers Scribner's to divert $8,000 from her royalties and offer them as an advance to James for 'an important American novel'. James was delighted at the largest advance he ever received, and never guessed the prompter of his publishers' urgent generosity (he never completed the book, *The Ivory Tower*, either).

Or you might prefer to approach a novel like *The Reef* on the lookout for a few key words. Here are some of them:

Natural. At the start of the novel George Darrow, an unmarried American diplomat of thirty-seven, ponders the contrasting appeals of Anna Leath, his early and now renewed love, and the passingly encountered Sophy Viner. Anna is widowed, rich and of good stock; Sophy is young, unattached, of unknown social origin but with bohemian connections. It appears to be a light-hearted contest (since Darrow knows his heart to be engaged in one direction only) between the charm of naturalness and the solider appeal of good manners. Sophy's forwardness and vivacity make companionship easy and immediate, giving Darrow's dealings with her a rare freshness; on the other hand, such naturalness has its drawbacks, notably a tendency to provoke embarrassment. Her initial and prime effect is to show up the world of Darrow and Anna in all its evasive formality; it makes him reflect on 'the deadening process of forming a "lady"' in good society. Travelling to Paris on the train with Sophy, Darrow indicates the term which is the novel's polar opposite to 'naturalness'. Had he been in the same compartment and circumstances with Anna, he decides, she would not have been so restless and talkative; she would have behaved 'better' than Sophy, 'but her adaptability, her appropriateness, would not have been nature but "tact"'. Sophy strikes him as having the naturalness of 'a dryad in a dew-drenched forest'; but – regrettably, or fortunately – we no longer live in forests, and 'Darrow reflected that mankind would never have needed to invent tact if it had not first invented social complications'.

Sophy's Parisian plan is to train for the stage, and her open, intelligent, frank, naive and unfettered approach to things – her naturalness – probably persuades the reader that this would be a fitting career. But Darrow is shrewder than the reader: in his experience the vivacity of an actress onstage is quite different from the vivacity of a person in life; the latter does not assist the former. To Darrow, Sophy seems 'destined to work in life itself rather than any of its counterfeits'. Here he proves correct: he recognises that Sophy is unequal to either kind of counterfeiting – that of the actress, or that involved in 'the deadening process of forming a "lady"'.

At this stage of the novel, the viewpoint and the judgements are Darrow's, the rivalry between 'naturalness' and 'tact' seen through his eyes. It is always clear, however, to which world Darrow – a diplomat by instinct as well as profession – belongs. Much later in the novel, Anna is trying to understand the earlier appeal of Sophy Viner to the man she loves, envying those who have 'plunged', trying to understand the 'darkness' of her own heart and to release her own sexuality. She is aware of Sophy's advantage over her. In this condition she views Darrow's handling of women with a disenchanted eye, and turns against him the word he had earlier used against (though also in praise of) her: 'The idea that his tact was a kind of professional expertise filled her with repugnance, and insensibly she drew away from him.'

Veil. What is the consequence of 'tact', of the dread process of 'forming a lady'? It is to place a veil between the self and the emotions. One of the most powerfully compacted and ironic lines of the novel comes when Anna, musing on the social rules of the world in which she grew up, recollects that 'people with emotions were not visited'. At that time, and during her subsequent marriage to Leath, the veil between herself and life 'had been like the stage gauze which gives an illusive air of reality to the painted scene behind it, yet proves it, after all, to be no more than a painted scene'. This is a cunning image: the veil is not just a barrier between herself and life, but something actively deceptive – behind it is not reality but a theatrical fake. To translate the metaphor: social training gives you the illusion that a stodgy dried-up snuffbox-collecting bore of a husband is a rightful object of romantic attachment. Anna's story is about the rending of the veil between herself and life; the point about the veil being that, once rent, it cannot be unrent.

Life. Hardly a word one might expect to be unimportant in a novel. But here it is especially charged: the word – the thing – focuses the struggle between tact and naturalness. Darrow, we are told early on, has a 'healthy enjoyment of life'; Anna is 'still afraid of life'; whereas Sophy has the word 'often on her lips' – even if, in Darrow's view, when she speaks about 'life' she seems 'like a child playing with a tiger's cub; and he said to himself that some day the child would grow up – and so would the tiger'.

Darrow has an attitude to life; Sophy *is* an attitude to life. It is within Anna that the novel's great psychological drama takes place: a struggle to understand what is, or could be, life, whether it is a wonderful or a terrible thing, and what the price of such understanding might be. She has been brought up in Old New York and transplanted to old provincial France: during her marriage she discovered that 'real life', that glib phrase, was for her 'neither dead nor alive'. Later, in her widowhood, she supports her stepson Owen's desire to marry an 'unsuitable girl', aware that his rebellion is also hers – even if it is a kind of retrospective rebellion, a refutation of her earlier timorousness and tact. During this first, proxy engage-ment in the cause of life she can afford to be dashing and freethinking. The real struggle lies ahead: with what Sophy represents in terms of womanhood, modernity and sexuality; with the responses such women provoke in Darrow and other men; with her own emotional and sexual repression. The choice – all the harder since she is not Sophy's age – seems to be between living a restricted existence with her head held high and eyes averted, and 'looking at life' with all its consequent agony. Even so, how can she be sure that the tormenting predicament into which she has been thrust is indeed 'life'? Anna's big question, asked at the end of Chapter 30, is whether 'life' is really 'like that' – i. e. 'grotesque and mean and miserable' – or whether her 'adventure' is a 'hideous accident'.

Metaphors of sturdy usefulness accumulate around the word 'life' in *The Reef*. For Leath, life 'was like a walk through a carefully classified museum'; for Anna, while married to him, 'it was like groping about in a huge dark lumber-room where the exploring ray of curiosity lit up now some shape of breathing beauty and now a mummy's grin'. When Darrow appears to be rescuing her, she tells him, 'I want our life to be like a house with all the windows lit; I'd like to string lanterns from the roof and chimneys!' Later, when the rescue has proved more life-threatening than anticipated, she employs a broader architectural metaphor: 'She looked back with melancholy derision on her old conception of life, as a kind of well-lit and well-policed suburb to dark places one need never know about.' But the truth of the novel does not support this town-planning notion of existence. Rather, it is on the side of Darrow's comparison of life to a tiger's cub which grows up. Life's instincts are destructive, not constructive. Or as Darrow pompously explains it to Anna:

> When you've lived a little longer you'll see what complex blunderers we all are: how we're struck blind sometimes, and mad sometimes – and then, when our sight and our senses come back, how we have set to work, and build up, little by little, bit by bit, the precious things we'd smashed to atoms without knowing it. Life's just a perpetual piecing together of broken bits.

The metaphor here is less precise, no doubt deliberately so. We might imagine the destruction of an idol, icon or statue; except that 'broken bits' sounds more like pottery – at which point we might recall that Darrow had earlier compared his pursuit of the elusive Anna to the figures on a Grecian urn, vainly chasing one another throughout eternity. Now the urn is in shards. Of course, when people talk of 'life' they rarely do anything but generalise from their own experience; so we could take Darrow's assertion that 'Life's just a perpetual piecing together of broken bits' less as authorial conclusion than as special pleading by the man who dropped the pot.

House. If Anna wants her life with Darrow to be like a house with all the windows lit, we cannot help noticing that she has one of these already. And what a house Givré sounds, lovingly described by Wharton. At best it seems to give off a moral force, with 'the high decorum of its calm lines and soberly massed surfaces'. But the house is more a mutable character in the novel than a monolithic point of reference; 'decorum' is very close to 'tact', and the same building may, in other moods, come to represent 'the very symbol of narrowness and monotony'. A house implies a habitat; this novel is about being emotionally 'unhoused' – having your roof blown off.

Racinian. This word does not appear in *The Reef*, but has been associated with it from early on. Writing to thank the author for her novel in December 1912, Henry James offered this praise: 'The beauty of it is that it is, for all it is worth, a Drama and almost, as it seems to me, of the psychologic Racinian unity, intensity and gracility.' The same adjective had been applied a little earlier by Charles du Bos, the French translator of *The House of Mirth*, who told Wharton after reading the proofs of *The Reef* that 'No novel came closer to the quality of a tragedy of Racine.' It is true that there are a small number of characters; that the action (after Book I) takes place in an enclosed area; that a complex and intensifying emotional predicament unfolds, binding in ever more tightly the four main characters, so that none can move, or lie, or tell the truth, without a dire chain of consequences – as Anna tells Darrow, 'We're all bound together in this coil.' But we should allow for the tendency of French translators to Gallicise as they applaud; and also that of friendly novelists to approve those aspects of a work which seem most to resemble aspects of their own. The critical line on *The Reef*, started by James's approval, is that it is Wharton's most Jamesian – specifically late-Jamesian – novel. Though there are undeniable echoes of the Master, it's worth remembering that Wharton consistently disliked late James, finding an airlessness in the very sense of enclosure here applauded.

And by Racinian, should we understand also 'tragic'? Probably not: when the coil finally comes unbound, Sophy is returned to the social and financial position she was in before the novel began, Anna and Darrow get a tarnished version of what they had wanted, while Owen runs away (having at least been spared a perilous marriage). There has, it is true, been a tremendous smash, and the lives of these four will never be the same again: Anna's unenviable final choice is between the long misery of giving Darrow up and the equally long misery of living with someone whose words you cannot trust. However, compared to, say, that other great and near-contemporary novel of coil-bondage, Ford Madox Ford's *The Good Soldier* (1915), there is a very low body count.

It is probably the case that the tragic no longer exists in modern life, or therefore in the modern novel. We may take the starting point of the latter as *Madame Bovary*, a work whose influence on Wharton is apparent; also a novel which defines the diminished version of the tragic nowadays allowable – a ruthless chain of events made more ruthless by the rules and forms of society, and also by the expectations, misconceptions and self-destructiveness of the principal character. Ford's novel does not begin 'This is the most tragic story I have ever heard' but 'This is the saddest story I have ever heard.' One reason for this is that the gods have been replaced. When Darrow takes Sophy to see a French version of *Oedipus*, the characters make her feel 'as if the gods were there all the while, just behind them, pulling the strings'. In the absence of these controlling gods, we have the vain illusion that it is *we*, with our famous free will, who pull the strings. *The Reef* is a novel which doubts this: as Darrow remarks to Sophy at the start of it all, 'What rubbish we talk about intentions!' And so we do: they are an attempt to impose purpose and rationality upon the flapping laundry of our emotional lives. Darrow invokes the world of Greek tragedy again at the end of the novel, during his key exchange with Anna (Chapter 32). He asks: 'Is it anything to be proud of, to know so little of the strings that pull us?' This is the measure of our aloneness, our lack of tragic stature: we are still puppets twitched by strings, but the puppeteer's box up there is no longer occupied.

Luck. In tragedy, this used to be called destiny. In our reduced state, we find a lesser word for it. In *The Reef*, the term is attached to Sophy Viner (this is appropriate, for the world of 'tact' she is about to explode with her presence does not acknowledge luck much: to do so would be a denial of merit, birth, rank, money).

> Darrow perceived that she classified people according to their greater or less 'luck' in life, but she appeared to harbour no resentment against the undefined power which dispensed the gift in such unequal measure. Things came one's way or they didn't . . .

Though Sophy is unschooled in the classics, when she watches *Oedipus* her role as luck detector enables her to touch the play's pulse, to feel 'the ineluctable fatality of the tale, the dread sway in it of the same mysterious "luck" which pulled the threads of her own small destiny'. Of course, by the time

Sophy lightly introduces this concept, the 'luck' that is to settle her fate and that of others has already happened. At first it appears mainly the fault of the postal services (always handily at a novelist's beck and call): if only Darrow hadn't had Anna's telegram flung into his compartment just as the boat-train was pulling out . . . If only Sophy had not left London so precipitately, before any letter from the Farlows detailing their changed plans could reach her . . . These are certainly factors: but when, hundreds of pages on, after the smash, Darrow is seeking to explain how his trivial, central liaison with Sophy began, he identifies a different hazardous aspect: 'Perhaps but for the rain it might never have happened.' He is referring specifically to the day in Paris when the rain makes them return to their hotel earlier than usual. But this in turn alerts the reader (though not Darrow) to earlier rain at Dover when he and Sophy encountered one another. He is scrambling around in a gale when 'a descending umbrella caught him in the collar-bone' – an impact, a first proleptic smash, which destroys Sophy's umbrella, and leads her to shelter beneath his. All the fault of the rain? In the old Greek days, the gods sent thunderbolts to determine our fates; now meteorologists guide our luck.

In the final chapter, Anna broods on whether she can free herself from the inevitability of life with George Darrow; and she becomes 'vaguely conscious that the inky escape from it must come from some external chance'. Anna, being posh, does not acknowledge luck except by a posher name; but she is correct in deducing that 'luck' somehow resides in Sophy Viner. If she can find Sophy and tell her she is renouncing Darrow, there will be no turning back on the decision and she will be free. Anna goes to Paris, but Sophy has already left for India, taking her luck – and Anna's 'external chance' – with her.

Reef. The word occurs monolithically as the title and we wait for its appearance in the text. We wait in vain. Towards the end of Book II marine metaphors seem to put us on watch: Darrow is taking a 'dark dive' into his difficulties; he feels the 'sweep of secret tides'; meanwhile, Sophy has been 'adrift', while Anna is 'floating' on a 'tide of felicity'. These aquatic hints lead nowhere for the moment. Later, Darrow feels the light of Anna's eyes moving before him 'as the sunset moves before a ship at sea'; later, again, Anna has a 'flood of pent-up anguish' – and the metaphor seems to have drained away into a formulaic phrase. But just as we might have given up expectations, Wharton craftily produces the held-back image – though not the word itself. Darrow, in his climactic scene with Anna, tries to explain how the smash came about: 'It seemed such a slight thing – all on the surface – and I've gone aground in it because it *was* on the surface.' Again, we might find the image masculine special pleading (Sophy as a largely inert lump of coral whose only function is to tear the hull out of smart pleasure boats). We might wonder if the metaphor had wider application, and is intended to denote the reef of Anna's sensual unresponsiveness, on which Darrow also goes aground. And we might wonder if Wharton, having left the image so late, might either have made more of it, or left it out altogether, letting the title do the work by itself. *The Reef* is unusual in Whartonian composition in that the proofs were delayed between America and France (the 'luck' of the postal services again), and she did not have time for her normal last-minute reassessment. What might she have altered?

Silence. The main action of *The Reef* consists of conversation and of ruminations preparatory to conversation (in 1921 Wharton wrote to Mary Cadwalader Jones, 'How odd that no one should know that there is a play in "The Reef" all ready to be pulled out!'). But as the novel proceeds, it becomes clear that what is not said – and the way in which it is not said – may be as telling as any words. 'Silence may be as variously shaded as speech,' Wharton comments. For instance,

Owen's suspicions about Sophy and Darrow's relationship are aroused precisely by the fact that when he spots them alone together they are always sunk in silence; had their relationship been as it was presumed, they would have been chatting in some normal social way. Equally, Darrow's 'not speaking', or withholding of an opinion, about Sophy stirs unintended doubts about her capability as a governess. And at the very start of things, when Darrow and Sophy are in Paris together, the moment in their acquaintanceship comes when 'the natural [*sic*] substitute for speech had been a kiss'. Sex as a way of not speaking – and also of 'not having to listen', as Darrow cruelly remembers. As at the start, so at the end, with Anna looking back over the disastrous chain of events which followed Darrow's first arrival at Givré:

> She perceived that at no time had anyone deliberately spoken or anything been accidentally disclosed. The truth had come to light by the force of its irresistible pressure . . . She felt anew the uselessness of speaking.

This is a profound realisation to fall upon lucid and sophisticated people, who use words to define the world, and also to manipulate it, to keep it at bay. 'The truth had come to light by the force of its irresistible pressure': perhaps there is an alternative metaphorical title to the novel lurking in here. There is also the recognition that in our own modern version of tragedy – less grand, yet more bleak – we are beyond nobility, beyond the string-pulling gods, beyond Racine, beyond luck, beyond help, beyond even words.

HOMAGE TO HEMINGWAY:
A SHORT STORY

1. The Novelist in the Countryside

THEY SAT INFORMALLY around a stripped-pine kitchen table. Behind him was a matching dresser, opposite him a picture window through which he could see a cluster of damp sheep, then rising pastureland which disappeared into low cloud. It had rained every one of the five days they'd been here. He wasn't sure this kind of communal living, which had sounded so jolly and democratic in the brochure, was for him. Of course, it was the students who were expected to cook, wash up and keep the place tidy; but since half of them were older than he was, it would have been stuffy not to muck in. So he stacked plates, made toast, and had even promised to cook them a big lamb stew on the final night. After supper they would put on their waterproofs and slog a mile down the track to a pub. Each evening he seemed to need a little more drink than before to keep him stable.

He liked his students, with their earnestness and optimism, and asked them to call him by his Christian name. All did so, except for Bill, a rather truculent ex-serviceman who preferred to address him as 'Chief'. Some of them, it was true, enjoyed literature more than they understood it, and imagined that fiction was merely autobiography with a tweak.

'I'm just saying, I don't understand why she did it.'

'Well, people often don't understand why they do things.'

'But we, as readers, should know, even if the character herself doesn't.'

'Not necessarily.'

'I agree. I mean, we don't believe any more in the, what did you call it, Chief?'

'Omniscient narrator, Bill.'

'That's the ticket.'

'All I'm saying is, there's a difference between not believing in an omniscient narrator and not understanding what's going on in a character's head.'

'I said people often don't understand why they do things.'

'But look, Vicky, you're writing about a woman with two small children and what sounds like a perfectly OK husband who suddenly ups and kills herself.'

'So?'

'So, maybe – maybe – there's a question of plausibility.'

He could feel tempers rising, but was disinclined to interrupt. He preferred to muse on the question of plausibility. Take his own case. Or rather, his and Angie's. They'd been together seven years, she'd shared every day of his struggle to become a writer, he'd produced his first novel, she'd seen it published and well reviewed – it had even won a prize – whereupon she had dumped him. He understood women leaving men because they were failures, but leaving him because he was a success? Where was the motivation in that? Where was the plausibility? Conclusion, one among many: don't try putting your own life into fiction. It won't work.

'Are you saying my story's implausible?'

'Not exactly, I was just –'

'You don't believe such women exist?'

'Well –'

'Because, let me tell you, they *do*.' (Vicky's voice now had a tremble to it.) 'That woman, that woman you don't think is plausible, that woman's *my mother*, and I can tell you that she was plausible enough to me in real life, when she was alive.'

There was a long silence. Everyone was looking at him, expecting him to take charge. Which he would, of course, though not by sitting in judgement, rather by telling them a story. It was a stratagem he'd devised on the first morning – of throwing into each session an anecdote, a memory, a long joke, even a dream. He never explained why he was doing it, but each free-form intervention was designed to make them ask: is this a story? If not, how might we turn it into one? What do we need to discard, what keep, what develop?

And so he told them about going to Greece, perhaps a dozen years previously, back in the late sixties. It was the first time he'd been in a country whose language he couldn't understand at all. Friends had rented a house on Naxos for three weeks. It was high summer, and six hours on open deck from Piraeus had left him with a sunburn that made him nauseous and kept him indoors for the first two days. The few other foreigners on the island were as conspicuous as this little English group must have been. In particular; he remembered an American, a chunky fellow with white hair and a short-trimmed white beard; he wore a loose white shirt over belted shorts and drove a white jeep or buggy which was equally at home on the beach as on the coastal road. He would roar past, one leg out on the running board, one arm around a woman – late thirties, perhaps – with olive skin and black hair dyed an unconvincing blonde. She was evidently an island woman, and the prim young Englishman he'd been (but implicitly was no longer) had concluded that she was the island whore, rented by the week at perhaps the same rate as the jeep; or, indeed, with the jeep as a package. Occasionally, they would see the couple in a bar or restaurant, but mostly they were in motion, showing off. The fellow had clearly been modelling himself on Hemingway, and the prim Englishman, both impressed and disgusted by the macho swagger, had hated him on sight. Every time the

jeep came past them on the beach, even if it was far away, it
seemed to be throwing sand in his face.

He left it at that, hoping that his students would reflect
on the assumptions we automatically make about people –
even up to the possibility that the couple were happily married
tourists, and the husband had always dressed and worn his
beard like that. He also hoped they would reflect on life's
influence on art, and then art's influence back on life. And if
they had asked, he would have replied that for him, Hemingway,
as a novelist, was like an athlete bulked up on steroids.

'OK, all of you, now tell me what's wrong with the
following line: "Her voice was as beautiful as Pablo Casals
playing the cello"?'

He didn't tell them it was from *Across the River and into
the Trees*, a novel that epitomised for him the worst of
Hemingway. At university, he and his friends had taken to
mocking the line, inserting the names of other cellists, other
instruments, other physical attributes. Her breasts were as
beautiful as Stéphane Grappelli playing the jazz violin, and so
on. It had been a game which ran and ran.

'I think that's rather nice.'

'It's showing off, like he's hitting us around the head with
high culture.'

'Did I say it was written by a man?'

'It's obvious. Any woman can tell.'

He nodded as if to allow a palpable hit.

'Why does the writer say "Pablo", why not just "Casals"?'

'Perhaps to distinguish him from Rosie Casals?'

'Who's Rosie Casals?'

'A tennis player.'

'Sorry, did she play the cello as well?'

And so they got through the morning. They were a nice
bunch, all eight of them: five women and three men. A poet
friend of his had suggested that creative writing courses were
basically sex academies where the tutor automatically enjoyed

jus primae noctis. But perhaps aspirant poets were different from their prose equivalents. There was one woman on the course to whom he might happily have offered private lessons, but he gave up on the idea after spotting her arm in arm with Talentless Tim, who defended his consistent use of cliché by saying, 'It's not cliché, it's vernacular.'

They were settling in at the pub, pulling chairs together, when Bill slapped his palm on the table.

'Hey, Chief, I've just had a thought. What if it *was* Hemingway, the man himself, on that island of yours?'

'Not unless suicides come back from the dead.'

Oh shit, he thought, looking around to see if Vicky had heard. Luckily, she was at the bar buying her round. Trying to seem casual, he asked if any of them had read Hemingway. There were only two yeses, both from men. But everyone knew something about the writer's life – bullfighting, big-game hunting, expatriate in Paris, war correspondent, many wives, drinking, suicide – and so everyone, from this knowledge, had an opinion about the work. The sum of which was: a writer whose era had passed, and whose opinions were now out of date. Vicky began a long rant about cruelty to animals, and yes, perfectly on cue, Bill asked her if her shoes were made of leather.

'Yes, but it didn't come out of the bullring.'

And so he listened and smiled and drank some more. At the pub, he stopped being a tutor; they could say what they liked.

On the last evening, he cooked a gigantic stew and provided so many bottles of wine that they didn't need the pub. Responding to their praise, he told them his theory of writers and cooking. Novelists, who were in it for the long haul, were temperamentally equipped for stewing and braising, for the slow mixing together of many ingredients; whereas poets ought to be good at stir-fry. And short-story writers? someone asked. Steak and chips. Dramatists? Ah, dramatists

– they, the lucky sods, were basically mere orchestrators of the talents of others, so would be satisfied with shaking a leisurely cocktail while the kitchen staff rustled up the grub.

This went down well, and they started fantasising about the sort of food famous writers would serve. Jane Austen and Bath buns. The Brontës and Yorkshire pudding. There was even an argument when Virginia Woolf and cucumber sandwiches were put together. But without any discord they placed Hemingway in front of an enormous barbecue piled with marlin steaks and cuts of buffalo, a beer in one hand and an outsized spatula in the other, while the party swirled around him.

The next morning, they shared a minibus to the local station. The rain still hadn't given up. At Swansea there were handshakes and some shy cheek-kissing, and the woman he'd fancied gave him a look which seemed to be saying: no, didn't you see, it wasn't Tim I would have gone for, I only put my arm through his because I felt sorry for him. All you had to do was look at me properly, make some kind of sign. He wondered if this was a correct conclusion based on his sympathetic imagination, or merely mad vanity. But in any case, she was now on a different train, heading towards a different life, while he sat at the window on his own, looking out at wet Wales. He found himself thinking that, driver aside, a white beach buggy had an unquestionable glamour about it. If you drove one round London, people would probably think you a member of a rock group rather than a mere prose writer. The pity was, he couldn't afford one. All he could afford was a second-hand Morris Minor.

2. The Professor in the Alps

He sat at the head of a long, dark table with six students at precise intervals down each side. Fifteen feet away, at the other end, was Guenther, his teaching assistant, whose broad shoulders and cheerful sweater obscured a view of forest, looping cables and high mountains. It was mid-July: the ski shops and hire places were closed, as were half the restaurants. There were a few tourists, some groups of hikers, and this summer school, which had invited him to teach – in English, fortunately – for six days. He was offered business-class travel, a decent fee, a healthy per diem, and use of the school's minivan whenever it was free. His only other obligation was to give a public reading on the final night. He was looking forward to this: his generation of writers had adapted well to the expectation that they become performers as well as private, solitary truth-seekers and truth-tellers. He was at ease with interviewers, usefully provocative on political issues – especially when he had a new book out – and a little whorish at the microphone. Ah, the lure of the prepared impromptu. This side of him had come as a surprise, pleasant to him, less so to Lynn, his wife, who had just left him. It had not been an agreeable time lately. 'And don't write a book about us like you did with Angie' had been one of her many parting lines. He had raised his hands, palms forward, as if to say that not only would he never do that, but it had been a clear mistake in the first case. Even if the novel had made a couple of shortlists. Even if fiction was, as he liked to say, omnivorous and essentially amoral.

'But what does the Herr Professor think about this?'

'I'd like to hear what the rest of you have to say first. Mario? Dieter? Jean-Pierre?'

He needed more time to think. It was an afternoon session which was intended to range more broadly. In the morning, they would analyse texts the students were to be examined on; in the afternoon he was expected to stretch their brains, make wider cultural connections, discuss social and political topics. It ought to have been a breeze, but there were times when their Continental minds, their natural ease with the abstract and the theoretical, made his own English pragmatism seem like mental sloppiness. Still, they liked him, and he liked them, not least because they seemed to ascribe his lack of rigour to the vibrancy of his imagination. He, they never forgot, was the Herr Professor, the one who had written the books. And if all else failed, he could always tell them an anecdote, a dream, a memory, a shaggy-dog story. They were very polite, and had heard about the famous English sense of humour, so anything he said that was at all odd, or incoherent, was greeted with respectful laughter.

But Jean-Pierre and Mario and Dieter had all delivered their opinions, and now it was up to him.

'Do any of you know the music of Sibelius?'

Only two. Good.

'Well, you must forgive me if I can't explain it in the correct musicological language. I'm only an amateur. Anyway, OK, Sibelius. 1865 approximately to 1957 approximately.' (He knew these were the exact dates – this was what he meant by 'whorish'.) 'Seven symphonies, one violin concerto, orchestral tone poems, songs, a string quartet called *Voces intimae*, intimate voices. Let's take the symphonies.' (Not least because he didn't have anything to say about the other works.) 'They start – the first two – with great melodic expansiveness. You hear a lot of Tchaikovsky, a bit of Bruckner, Dvořák perhaps, anyway, the great nineteenth-century European symphonic tradition. Then the Third – shorter, just as melodic, and yet more restrained, held-back, moving in a new direction. Then the great Fourth, austere, forbidding, granitic, the work where he most engages with modernism.' (He'd stolen that phrase from an Austrian pianist who said in a radio interview, 'No, Sibelius is not of much interest to me, except for the Fourth, where he engages with modernism.') 'Then the Fifth, Sixth, and that epitome of compression, the Seventh. To my doubtless fallible ears, one of the things Sibelius is asking, from the Third to the

Seventh is, What is melody? How far can we compress it, reduce it to a phrase, even, but make that phrase as charged and memorable as some Big Tune from the good old days? Music that seems to question itself and its underlying justification even as it beguiles you. I wish I could play you some.'

'Herr Professor, there is a piano in the conference hall.'

'Thank you, Guenther.'

He frowned as if his train of thought had been interrupted. His teaching assistant was always looking for ways to assist, which was logical, and yet at times disconcerting. Still, Guenther was very good at shameless queue-barging to fetch the Herr Professor his coffee.

'So what I suppose I am trying to say is: what is this thing – this ancient, wonderful thing – we call a story? This is a question modernism asked and, you could say, we all still need to ask. And when I consider that simple, essential question – what is narrative? – I often find myself turning to the mighty Finn. Sibelius' (he added in case they didn't know the composer was Finnish). 'Yes, Sibelius. Well, a break perhaps and, yes, thank you Guenther, and no milk.'

When they resumed, twenty minutes later, the teaching assistant arrived with a record player and several old LPs.

'I have the First Symphony, the Fourth and the Seventh, Herr Professor.'

'Guenther, you're a magician, how did you do it?'

His assistant smiled shyly. 'I found the name of a music professor in the village. He was delighted to lend you the records. He sends you his honoured greetings. The player belongs to the school.'

He was aware of the students looking at him expectantly.

'Well then. The first movement of the Fourth, if you don't mind.'

And so he sat and thought how wonderful it was to be

paid to listen to Sibelius, even if it was only for eight minutes and forty-seven seconds. How wonderful the music was too, how darkly orphic in this landscape of tall trees, clean air and blue sky. His life was a mess, his last novel had been crapped on from a great height by all the shitbags in London, he doubted he would ever write anything of lasting value, and yet – with those strings climbing timorously and the brass clearing its throat as if to make some great statement that was never, finally, made – there were still transcendent moments to be had in this poor existence of ours.

When the movement ended, he nodded at Guenther to lift the pickup. And just sat there, not saying a word, but trying to imply: I rest my case. Later, at supper, where everyone ate hugger-mugger, some of his students told him how much they had liked the music. In another mood, he might have taken this amiss, and presumed they were saying they didn't like something else – his way of teaching, his clothes, his opinions, his books, his life – but the music had delivered, if not a peacefulness, at least a quiet pause into his being. And more and more, he thought that was the best you could hope for in life: a kind of pause.

The next afternoon, he decided to tell them about Hemingway. He began with the man in the white jeep on Naxos, which over the years had become for him an emblematic warning of what happens when a writer's life takes over from a writer's art. Why would anybody want to go around pretending to be Hemingway? he asked. He didn't imagine there had ever been false Shakespeares in England, *ersatz* Goethes in Germany, *faux* Voltaires walking around France. They laughed at this, and had he known the Italian for 'fake', he would have thrown in Dante to please Mario.

He told them how for a long time he had disregarded Hemingway, but in recent years come to admire him greatly. The stories, rather than the novels: in his view, the Hemingway method worked better over the shorter distance. Well, it was the same with James Joyce. *Dubliners* was a masterpiece, but *Ulysses*, for all its opening brilliance, was essentially a short story on steroids, grotesquely bulked up. If *Ulysses* were entered for the Olympics, it would fail a drugs test. He liked this opinion of his, and the way it always caused disquiet – here more than usual, he noted.

But he wanted to direct them to a story called, appropriately, 'Homage to Switzerland'. Not among Hemingway's more famous stories, but one of his most formally inventive. It had a three-part structure. In each part, a man – an expatriate American – was waiting for a train at a different Swiss railway station. It was the same train they were all waiting for, and the men, though they had different names, were versions of one another, or, quite possibly – not literally, but metaphorically, fictionally – the same man. He was waiting in the station café because the train was late. He drank, he propositioned the waitress, he teased the locals. Something, we are meant to conclude, had happened in the American's life. Perhaps he is burnt out. Perhaps his marriage is in ruins. The train's destination is Paris: maybe he has been running away from something and is now returning to it. Or maybe his ultimate destination is America. So it was a story about flight and return home – also, perhaps, a flight from the self and a possible, hoped-for return to it. And the way the three parts of the story overlapped, just as the men overlapped and the bars overlapped and the train overlapped, made us think about the way our own lives overlapped with one another. How we are all connected, all complicit.

There was silence when he finished speaking. It was odd, he thought, how much easier it was to talk about something you hadn't reread for a while. You didn't get so bogged down in particularities – the wider truths of fiction seemed to emerge naturally as you spoke.

Eventually Karin, a quiet but determined Austrian girl, broke the silence.

'So, Herr Professor, you are telling us that Hemingway is just like Sibelius?'

He smiled enigmatically, and made the coffee sign to Guenther.

3. The Maestro in the Midwest

The only view was of classrooms and other offices, though if you pressed close to the window you could see discouraged grass below and sky above. From the start, he had declined to take his expected position at the head of the three metal tables that had been loosely bolted together. He would place the student whose work was being discussed at its head, and the principal critic, or responder, at its foot. He himself would sit a third of the way along one side. His positioning was designed to say: I am not the arbiter of truth, because there is no final truth in literary judgement. Of course, I am your professor, and have published several novels whereas you have only had stuff in campus magazines, but this doesn't necessarily make me your best critic. It may well be that the most useful assessor of your work will be found among your classmates.

This wasn't false modesty. He liked his students, all of them, and believed the feeling reciprocated; he'd also been surprised how each, regardless of ability, wrote with an individual voice. But everyone's critical sympathies only ran so far. Take Gun-boy, as he thought of him, who turned in nothing but Gen-X stories set in a rough part of Chicago, and who, when he didn't like someone else's work, would shape his hand into a revolver and 'shoot' them, adding the gesture of the gun's recoil for emphasis. No, he would never be Gun-boy's best reader.

It had been a good idea to come to this Midwestern campus, to remind himself of the normality and ordinariness of America. From a distance, the temptation was always to see it as a country which every so often went mad on power, and gave itself over to the violent outbursts of a steroid abuser. Here, away from the places and politicians which gave it that bad name, life was much like life everywhere else. People worried about the usual small things which to them were big things. As in his fiction. And here he was treated like a welcome guest, not a pariah, not a failure, but someone with his own life who had perhaps seen a few things they hadn't. Occasionally, there was a certain gulf in understanding: yesterday, he'd been sitting up at a lunch counter when his neighbour asked genially, 'So what language do they speak in Europe, then?' But such details would be useful for his American novel.

If he ever wrote it. No, of course he would write it. The question was: would anyone ever publish it? He had taken this job partly to escape the shame of having his last novel, *A Kind of Pause*, turned down by twelve publishers. And yet, he knew it wasn't a bad book. Everyone said it was as good as all his others – and therein lay the problem. His sales had been flatlining for years; he was white and middle-aged, with no other identity – smug TV panellist, for instance – to lift his profile. In his view, the novel – indeed, The Novel – delivered its rare truths through the artful mingling of intimate voices; yet nowadays people wanted something noisier. 'Perhaps I should kill my wife and then write a book about it,' he would complain in self-pitying moments. But he didn't have a wife, only an ex-wife towards whom he bore sentimental rather than murderous feelings. No, his novels were good, just not good enough, that was the truth. One publisher had written to his agent that *A Kind of Pause* was 'a classic, well-crafted mid-list book, the only trouble being that the mid-list doesn't exist any more'. His agent, with perhaps excessive candour, had passed the judgement on to him.

'Maestro?'

It was Kate, his cleverest student, even if she did have too many dogs in her stories. Once he had written in the margin in red biro 'Kill the dog'. The next story she had presented to the class was called 'The Immortal Dachshund'. He'd liked that. Teasing, he thought, could almost be as good as love, and sometimes better.

'I think you've covered all my points,' he said. Though his main point, had he been harsh enough to make it, would have been: why is this male take on existential angst so reminiscent of all the others you have submitted? But he didn't say things like that; he felt his students' vulnerability as if it were his own. Instead, since they were nearly halfway through the three-hour session, he simply called 'Cigarette Break.'

Often, he would join the class's three smokers in a huddle round a waste bin. Today, he strode off as if he had business elsewhere. Well, he did. He walked to the nearest edge of the campus, which was built on a rise, and looked out into the flat, inexpressive, agricultural distance. He didn't even need to light a cigarette. The view and its vast ordinariness were as good as nicotine. When he was young, he'd got satisfaction from imagining himself different from others, potentially special; now, he was comforted by reminders of his own – our own – insignificance. They calmed him.

Maestro. He grunted quietly to himself. When he first met the class, one of them had addressed him as 'Professor'. He'd jibbed at this – after all, he wasn't an academic, and preferred to think of himself as a writer among fellow writers. On the other hand, he didn't want them calling him by his Christian name. Some distance was necessary. And 'Mister——' didn't feel right either.

'Why don't we just call you Maestro?' Kate had suggested. He'd laughed. 'Only if you do so ironically.'

Now, he grunted again. At times, the label hurt. How proud he'd been to see his name on title page and book jacket, year after year. But what did that signify? Jane Austen's name was set in print only twice in her lifetime – and that in subscription lists for other people's books. Oh, enough, enough.

Every so often, to change the class's diet, he would hand out a short story he hoped would help them, or at least give a sense of perspective. So later that afternoon, he distributed Xeroxes of 'Homage to Switzerland'.

'Oh, Maestro,' Kate said, 'I can tell I'm going to be off sick next week.'

'You mean you have preconceptions?'

'Let's call them post-conceptions.'

He liked the way she held her own.

'For instance?'

She sighed. 'Oh, the ultimate dead white male. Papa Hemingway. The celebration of machismo. Boys with toys.' She deliberately looked at Gun-boy who, just as deliberately, took aim and shot her.

'Good. Now read the story.' And, in case she took offence, added, 'Dog-killer.'

The following week, he started by telling them about the Hemingway clone on the Greek island; then about the Swiss Alps and being asked whether he was comparing Hemingway with Sibelius. But this got little response, either because they hadn't heard of Sibelius, or – more likely – because he hadn't explained it properly. OK, over to them.

It depressed him how soon the class divided along sex lines. Steve, who was phobic about adverbs anyway, liked Hemingway's stylistic economy; Mike, whose formal high-jinks often concealed a paucity of subject matter, approved the structure; Gun-boy, perhaps deploring the lack of firearms, said the story was OK but didn't blow him away. Linda talked about the male gaze, and wondered why Hemingway hadn't given the waitresses names; Julianne found it repetitive. Kate, on whom he had been counting, tried to find praise but even she ended, wearily,

'I just don't see what he's got to say to us.'

'Then try listening more carefully.'

There was a shocked pause. He had turned on his favourite;

worse, he had stepped out of character. There was a tall poet on campus with a reputation for humiliating his students, destroying their poems line by line. But everyone knew poets were crazy and unmannerly. Prose writers, especially when foreign, were expected to be civil.

'I'm sorry. I apologise.'

But there was a tightness about Kate's face that made him feel guilty. It's not your problem, it's mine, he wanted to say. He thought of trying to explain something he had recently noticed about himself: that if anyone insulted him, or one of his friends, he didn't really mind – or not much, anyway. Whereas if anyone insulted a novel, a story, a poem he loved, something visceral and volcanic occurred within him. He wasn't sure what this might mean – except perhaps that he had got life and art mixed up, back to front, upside down.

But he didn't tell them this. Instead he began again, as if for the first time. He talked about the myth of the writer, and how it was not just the reader who became trapped in the myth, but sometimes the writer as well – in which case we should feel pity rather than blame. He talked about what hating a writer might mean. Did we hate Marlowe because he was a murderer? He quoted Auden on time pardoning Kipling for his views – 'And will pardon Paul Claudel, / Pardons him for writing well'. He confessed to his own early dislike for Hemingway, and how it had taken him a long time to read the words without seeing the man – indeed, this might be the most extreme example of the myth obscuring the prose. And how that prose was so different from the way it looked. It seemed to be simple, even simplistic, but at its best was as subtle and deep as anything by Henry James. He talked of Hemingway's humour, which was much overlooked. And of how, alongside what might appear to be boastfulness, there was often a surprising modesty and insecurity. Indeed, this was perhaps the key, the most important thing about the writer. People thought he was obsessed with male courage, with machismo and cojones. They didn't see that often his real subject was failure and weakness. Not the hero of the corrida but the humble aspirant stabbed to death by a bull made out of kitchen knives strapped to a chair. The great writers, he told them, understand weakness.

He left a pause, then turned back to 'Homage to Switzerland'. Note how the three-in-one American expatriate, despite wit, sophistication and money, is morally inferior to the simple Swiss waitresses and bar patrons, who are sturdily honest, who do not run from reality. Look at the moral balance sheet, he urged, look at the moral balance sheet.

'So why doesn't he give the women names?' Linda asked.

Which was coming out on top, irritation or depression? Perhaps there were some writers who would always be read and misread for the wrong reasons, who were, in fact, unrescuable. Auden, revising his work in later life, had cut those famous lines about Kipling and Claudel. Perhaps he came to believe them untrue, and that in the end time didn't pardon.

'They're waitresses. The story is seen through the eyes of an American outsider.'

'Who just wants to pay them for sex – as if they are whores.'

'Don't you see, the women have the high ground?'

'Then why not give one of them her own name?'

For a moment, he thought of telling them the story of his life: how Angie had left him because he was a success, and then Lynn had left him because he was a failure. But he didn't tell them that. Instead, he turned to Kate, in a final attempt at something – he wasn't even sure what – and asked,

'What if I wrote about this and gave my name and didn't give yours, would that really be bad?'

'Yes,' she replied, and it seemed to him that she now thought the less of him.

'And if I left out my name and gave yours, would that make it better?'

'Yes,' she said.

And so he did. He tried to write it all down, simply and honestly, with clean moral lines.

But still, nobody wanted to publish it.

LORRIE MOORE TAKES WING

LORRIE MOORE IS good at bad jokes. She's good at good jokes, too, and makes many of them. But good jokes are the sign of a certain control over the world, or at least of a settled vision, the sort of vision a writer has. Good jokes are finally just jokes; whereas bad jokes are more revelatory of character and situation. Wonky puns, look-at-me one-liners, inappropriately perky comebacks: these don't necessarily denote lack of humour, more a chin-up flailing at the discovery that the world is not a clean, well-lighted place; or that it is for some, but not for you, as the light falls badly on you and mysteriously casts no shadow.

Birds of America, Moore's third collection of stories, is cleverly laid out. It begins with seven stories of the kind at which she has always been supremely adept: shrewd, blackish tales of women on the edge of unravelling, smart women whose situations wouldn't be so bad if they weren't hopeless. The uncertainly married daughter on a motoring tour of Ireland with her seemingly hyper-efficient mother; the shy librarian trying to live with a political activist and finding personal commitment as hard and strange as the wider sort; the lawyer going home for a Christmas of relentless charades and sibling dysfunction; the wife and mother trying therapy for the death of her cat, having visited 'all the stages of bereavement: anger, denial, bargaining, Häagen-Dazs, rage'.

'She was unequal to anyone's wistfulness.' 'She hadn't been given the proper tools to make a real life with, she decided, that was it. She'd been given a can of gravy and a hairbrush and told, "There you go."' '*Blank* is to heartache as forest is to bench' (this, naturally, from a scholastic tester). 'She looked at Joe. Every arrangement in life carried with it the sadness, the sentimental shadow, of its not being something else, but only itself.' As a reviewer you are tempted merely to quote your way through this emotional territory, one in which sassy, or at least wryly percipient, women get involved with slower, generally well-meaning but finally hopeless men. Life constantly refuses to show such women the plot, or give them a big enough part, or allow them to wear enough make-up in the chorus line so as not to be recognised. Love? Love turns out to be 'flightless, dodo', and its fault lines no less painful for being familiar. When Olena the librarian (her name is already an anagram of Alone) discovers her lover is having an affair, his justification is so puny as to be almost winning: 'I'm sorry . . . it's a Sixties thing.' Simone, one of the robuster female characters, thinks that love affairs are like having raccoons in your chimney. How so?

> 'We have raccoons sometimes in our chimney . . .
> And once we tried to smoke them out. We lit a fire,
> knowing they were there, but we hoped that the
> smoke would cause them to scurry out the top and
> never come back. Instead, they caught on fire and
> came crashing down into our living room, all charred
> and in flames and running madly around until they
> dropped dead.' Simone swallows some wine. 'Love
> affairs are like that,' she says. 'They all are like that.'

There is serious pain at the edges of some of these stories (a child with cystic fibrosis, one with Down's syndrome), but the focus is on the tribulations – bitter, occasionally veering to bitter-sweet – of the thirty-something Midwestern female. The harsher critic, lolling in the front seats like an auditioning producer, might be tempted to point and growl, 'Fine, but what else can you do?' Whereupon Lorrie Moore proceeds to show us. The next two stories arrive from a male point of view (just in case we were wondering): an acrimonious academic dinner party ('Albert indicates in a general way where they should sit, alternating male, female, like the names of hurricanes'), and a road story about a blind lawyer and a hopeless house painter scratching their way round the South. From this point the stories grow bleaker ('He possessed a streak of pragmatism so sharp and deep that others mistook it for sanity') and invite broader extrapolation.

Before Audubon painted his *Birds of America*, we are reminded, he first shot them. There have been stray birds all through the book, bashing into windows, being tough on the dinner plate, flightlessly embodying love. Briefly, they now waddle centre stage, as the road couple attend the famous duck parade at the Peabody hotel in Memphis and watch 'these *rich, lucky* ducks' walk their red-carpeted way from foyer fountain to elevator. And what does this pampered life point up? That 'all the other birds of the world – the mange-hollowed hawks, the lordless hens, the dumb clucks – will live punishing, unblessed lives, winging it north, south, here, there, searching for a place of rest'.

The tonality becomes darkest in the last three stories, lit by bright truths to drive you mad. A woman in a traumatised remission from cancer; a baby with cancer; a woman who has accidentally killed a child and retreated from the deed into sudden marriage. But marriage has never been much of a haven in Mooreland, as its endurers report. 'The key to marriage, she concluded, was just not to take the thing too personally.' 'Marriage, she felt, was a fine arrangement generally, except that one never got it generally. One got it very, very specifically.' Marriage, another character notes, is an institution – as in mental institution. As for cancer: we are reminded of the title story in Moore's last collection, in which a woman is told that a mole removed from her back is pre-cancerous.

"'*Pre*-cancer,' she repeats. "Isn't that . . . like life?'"

'People Like That Are the Only People Here' was the story I was most eager, but also most anxious, to reread. Eager because the subject matter – a baby with cancer – takes Moore into her toughest territory, where every pitch of tone, let alone any joke, good or bad, looks the most exposed. Anxious because when the *New Yorker* first published the story, they chose to illustrate it with a very large and fetching photograph of Moore herself. Since, in the story, the baby's unnamed mother is a writer and a teacher living in the 'Modern Middle West', as Moore does, the magazine was inciting its readers, despite the 'fiction' strap, to treat it as a true-life account. This skewed the story and did Moore a disservice. In *Birds of America* it is freed into fiction; the rest of the book supports it, indeed builds towards it.

This doesn't make it any the less precisely harrowing. What, after all, could be more cosmically bad-jokey than the world of Peed Onk, that jaunty, demystifying reduction of Paediatric Oncology? Here are parents preparing to bury little children, unable to take upon themselves the pain of their little bald boys (statistically, it tends to be boys), moving between guilt and terror, between tormented relaxation in the cramped Tiny Tim Lounge (which would have been larger had Tiny Tim's child survived, rather than died, at the hospital) and the curt professional lingo of the staff: 'It's a fast but wimpy tumour,' the oncologist remarks consolingly. Reflecting on the experience, the mother wonders, 'How can it be described? . . . The trip and the story of the trip are always two different things.' True, as elsewhere; and Moore gives 'People Like That Are the Only People Here' some light metafictional embellishments to emphasise this. But the story can only work – as it compellingly does – if it is loyal to the full tonality of the original trip, articulating its terrors and banalities, its boredom and its death-defying jokes.

Lorrie Moore has always been a clever, witty writer. The

experimentalism of her early career seems currently in abeyance; *Birds of America* is formally conservative (indeed, in only one of the stories is the main narrative even intercut with a subsidiary one). As against that, her emotional range has deepened, and the sharp vignettes of her first work have yielded to the richer thirty- or forty-page narrative. Talent and promise often remain just that, throughout a career: Truman Capote had remarkable talent and promise all his life. Moore retains the avian eye of her early books, and an unwavering sense of social tone; she is thankfully still clever and witty, but her depth of focus has increased, and with it her emotional seriousness. I hesitate to lay the adjective 'wise' on one of her age. But watching a writer move into full maturity is always exciting. Flappy-winged take-off is fun; but the sight of an artist soaring lifts the heart.

REMEMBERING UPDIKE,
REMEMBERING RABBIT

I

HEARING OF JOHN Updike's death, I had two immediate, ordinary reactions. The first was a protest – But
I thought we had him for another ten years; the
second, a feeling of disappointment that Stockholm had never
given him the nod. The latter was a wish for him, and for
American literature; the former a wish for me, for us, for
Updikeans around the world. Though it was not as if he
hadn't left us enough to read. For years now his lifelong
publishers Knopf have been giving back-flap approximations.
In the mid-nineties, in a cute philoprogenitive linking, he
was 'the father of four children and the author of more than
forty books'. By the time of *Early Stories* (2003) they had
him, in a hands-in-the-air sort of way, as 'the author of fifty-
odd previous books'. Now, with *Endpoint*, his final collection
of poems, they award him 'more than sixty books'. Why ask
for another ten years and another ten books, when even
devoted Updikeans have probably only read half or two-thirds
of the corpus? (I have only met one person – a British arts
journalist – who has actually read *all* Updike's books.)
Nicholson Baker's act of homage, *U & I* (1991), was impu-
dently predicated on the fact that he'd by no means read all
of Updike, or fully remembered what he had – and no, he

wasn't going to do any extra homework before paying his tribute. It was a quirky approach, with which fellow Updikeans would sympathise; even if it did dangerously invite the act of imitation. I enjoyed Baker's book, without feeling obliged to read it all.

But Updike's fertility was matched by his courtesy – both as a man and as an authorial presence. His fiction never set out to baffle or intimidate – although he certainly could intimidate. Philip Roth, with memorably mock-aggrieved generosity, said of *Rabbit is Rich*:

> Updike knows so much, about golf, about porn, about kids, about America. I don't know anything about anything. His hero is a Toyota salesman. Updike knows everything about being a Toyota salesman. Here I live in the country and I don't even know the names of the trees. I'm going to give up writing.

Yet Updike always treated the reader as a joint partner in the artistic process, an adult equal with whom curiosity and delight in the world were to be shared. Departing, he left us not just one extra book, but two. It was an act of courtesy, but also of necessity. While Updike breathed, he wrote, and his entranced attentiveness to the world continued all the way to his deathbed. His final utterances, poems specifically dated from '11/02/08' to '12/22/08', are about hospital life, pneumonia, dead friends, needle biopsy, CAT-scan, 'endpoint'; and the tone and truthfulness of this last looking-around –

> *Days later, the results came casually through:*
> *The gland, biopsied, showed metastasis.*

– are both exemplary to any writer and infinitely touching to any long-term reader.

After the first shock of death came the admission that even a Nobel could guarantee only temporary permanence. (In *Bech is Back,* Izzy asks Bech if he's ever wanted to be a literary judge. "'No,' Bech admitted. "I always duck it." "Me, too. So who accepts? Midgets. So who do they choose for the prize? Another midget."') Then began a cautious, provisional assessment among Updikeans as to which of those 'more than sixty books' would remain after the inevitable historical shakedown. The Rabbit Quartet and the stories, most agree; beyond that, there is little unanimity. If *Couples* is his most famous single title, it is also his most contested; opponents might argue that *The Maples Stories* add up to a swifter, sparer analysis of American marriage in the same period. There are votes for *Of the Farm* and *The Coup* (my own would go to *Roger's Version*). The man himself said (in 1985, anyway) that his own 'particular favourite' was the very atypical (because intrusively metaphorical) *The Centaur*. Updike's later work was rather undervalued, and at times insultingly reviewed; perhaps *In the Beauty of the Lilies* will stay the course, or *Terrorist* (2006). The latter book has as much authorial boldness as Roth's *The Plot Against America*, even if both share the same unwillingness to push the narrative to its logical conclusion (the Roth would thus end with the setting-up of the first American concentration camp, the Updike with the successful blowing-up of the Lincoln Tunnel). As Lorrie Moore put it, Updike is 'arguably our greatest writer without a single great novel' – a matter of particularity rather than any dishonour.

Updike's stories were generally written closer to his own life than his novels; and his final collection, *My Father's Tears,* contains numerous familiar tropes, set-ups and situations. The infant crouched on carpet or linoleum, surrounded by crayons and mammoth adults; the child of a quadrilateral household (two parents, two grandparents) which cossets and protects him; the small boy losing his mother's hand in a department store and wetting his pants; the artistic yet temperamental mother and the philistine yet stoical father; the key move from town (the father's locale) to farm (the mother's); the necessary escape from family to university, then professional life and marriage; the fathering of four children; the period of a year or so living alone in Boston; divorce, followed by a second, childless marriage; the young man with psoriasis who grows into the elderly man with sun-damaged skin; the adult whose stutter returns in times of crisis or embarrassment; the serial attender of high-school reunions; the grandfather with a tendency to get lost, whether in foreign cities or his own once-familiar, now forever-changed home environment. These set-ups are so consistent that when, in 'Blue Light' (ex-psoriatic grandfather with sun-damaged skin), Updike proposes a protagonist with a massive three wives and a measly three children, we rear back not so much in disbelief as mild offence. Think we can't see through *that*? Anyway, three plus three or two plus four, it's still six, isn't it?

At the same time, the very existence of such solid tropes will make Updikeans hope that their man gets a non-reductivist biographer; it is what he does with his givens, not the identifiability of their origin, that counts. Thus, 'Blue Light' starts with Fritz Fleischer's visit to a dermatologist who advises a new treatment to flush out pre-cancerous cells. Yet each establishing detail proposes the story's wider concerns – damage and its lingering consequences ('the skin remembers', Fleischer's previous dermatologist has told him), the infliction of pain, genetic inheritance and ageing (with pre-cancerous cells, '"Maturing" seemed to be a euphemism for death'). It spins out into a story about 'personal archaeology' (as another title has it), about memory and family, innocence and age, selfishness and its consequences. The last two sentences stitch the story closed with a neat suture: 'He could not imagine what his grandchildren would do in the world, how they would earn their keep. They were immature cells, centers of potential pain.'

The younger writer is avid for the world and its description; the older writer, while still avid for description, is more suspicious about the world, both what it is and whom it might be for: 'It had taken old age', the narrator of 'The Full Glass' reflects, 'to make me realise that the world exists for young people.' But the older writer has also realised the extent and limitations of his own myth-kitty, and learned how best to eke it out. Those early memories which famously come back in old age are too precious to be wasted on just a single-layer, hey-look-what-I've-just-remembered story. The older writer (well, an older writer like Updike) has also learned how to move through time, a much harder task in the short story than in the novel. Not just the technicality of fast-forward and rewind, freeze-frame and wide shot, but the psychology of how memories of quick youth fit in with – or disturb – the slower travails of age, how we live not just in the present indicative but also the passive, the conditional and the subjunctive ('German Lessons'), how guilt works in the long haul, how unexpectedly some things still move us while others trigger nothing, and how far we can admit that our deepest and most companionable certainties were often wrong.

Updike's world often appears a superficially stable place, of mainly white, mainly middle-class suburbia, of houses and families and children and golf and drinking and, of course, adultery – that most conventional way to rise above the conventional, in Nabokov's phrase. But just as Hemingway, the supposed hymner of masculine courage, writes best about cowardice, so Updike, delineator of conventional, continuing America, is incessantly writing about flight. For the small, carpet-level boy with the dominant mother in 'The Guardians', 'crayoning was Lee's way of getting away from her'. Later will come the actual, necessary escape from the family (see the great early story 'Flight'), an action usually leading to marriage and a new family. That would have been the end of it for the generation of Updike's parents: in a pre-Elvis, pre-pill, still-puritan America, escape was theoretically possible but rarely feasible. For the next generation, it is not just an occasional dream but a constant possibility – though never a simple one. Little Lee, for instance, is comforted by the fact that his parents and grandparents do not die until he is 'safely away' at college. This is, perhaps, the underlying, paradoxical dream of Updike's characters: to be away, and yet to be safe. The Rabbit Quartet is bookended by Harry Angstrom's two instinctive southerly fugues: his opening panicked drive from home and family and life in the '55 Ford in *Rabbit, Run* ('The title can be read as advice,' Updike noted in his preface to the one-volume edition of the Quartet); and the mirror trip in *Rabbit at Rest*, Harry's closing, migratory trek in the Toyota Celica down to Florida to find his place to die. Updike's epitomal marrieds, the Maples, try the easiest escape from marriage, adultery, then the second one, divorce. But what lies beyond? A second marriage, perhaps further dreams of leaving, and so on, until life's final escape, into death. If Lee, at the end of 'The Guardians', finds temporary consolation in the fact that his DNA at least promises him longevity, Martin Fairchild, in 'The Accelerating Expansion of the Universe', knows that in cosmological terms, 'We are riding an aimless explosion to nowhere'.

What can't be escaped from, and which runs all through this final collection of stories, is memory. The escapee must always return, mentally or physically, if not both. In 'The Road Home', David Kern (to whom most tropes apply) goes back to his mother's farmland and his father's townscape, places from which 'only he' among all his family 'had escaped'. He has the hesitant nostalgia of the returnee, and also the guilt: if the place has changed unacceptably, then he himself, by his chosen absence, will be complicit in its decline. The past is somewhere you get lost in, literally and figuratively: your memory is partial, and the place itself has changed. And so have you: Kern, a city slicker worrying that rain-sodden fields might dirty his shoes and trousers, makes the discovery that 'ancestral soil' for him 'was just mud'. And sometimes not even that. The boy who once humiliatingly sold strawberries on the roadside of Route 14 sees how the fruit are grown today: under season-defying plastic, four feet off the ground, and hydroponically, with nutrients trickled in by hose. If the 'ancestral' has lost its meaning, so too has the 'soil'.

The final paradox and contradiction of escape is laid out in 'Free'. Henry and Leila, small-town adulterers who never made the break together, meet up again in their sixties. Henry's wife has died, and Leila, now out of her third unsatisfactory marriage, is living in a Florida condo with 'metal furniture and mall-bought watercolours'. Visiting her there after thirty years – and an hour overdue, since Henry, a true late-Updike male, is disoriented by directions – he finds her wrinkled from the sun, sharper-tongued and more vulgar than he remembered, sassy rather than cute. He is also disconcerted that there is both more time and more conversation than back in the old days, when 'Fuck and run had always been his style'. These changed circumstances make him indecisive, and when he defeatedly suggests getting back to his hotel, Leila has to coax him into bed with, 'You were always getting back . . . but you're free now.' Yet with time comes not just memory but reassessment. Afterwards, as he prepares for a long drive into a setting sun, Henry asks, 'Well, what is free? . . . I guess it's a state of mind. Looking back at us – maybe that was as free as things get.'

Here come the desolating consolations of age. Escape may not lead to freedom; the skin remembers; the body rebels. Even adultery, that old reliable, becomes less commanding an impulse, easily loses its thrall. In 'Outage', a near-infidelity during a power failure is comically headed off when the electricity returns, house lights suddenly blaze, and domestic machinery begins distractingly to hum and bleep. In 'The Apparition', Henry Milford, a retired professor in his seventies, half-bored on a cultural tour of India, falls into 'a default alliance of wilful ignorance' with a younger married woman. But – perhaps because of a lifetime spent teaching 'statistics and probabilities' – he is satisfied with merely savouring 'lust's folly' from a distance; the pleasures of the flesh being illustrated instead by a temple's erotic statuary.

Not all is retrospect: 'Varieties of Religious Experience' (first published in the *Atlantic* in November 2002) is Updike's initial response to 9/11, and thus a partial precursor to *Terrorist*. Dan Kellogg, a 63-year-old Episcopalian staying with his daughter in Brooklyn Heights, realises that there is no God the instant he watches the South Tower fall. He is puzzling over the oily smoke from the buildings 'when, as abruptly as a girl letting fall her silken gown, the entire skyscraper dropped its sheath and vanished, with a silver rippling noise'. It is a comparison few except Updike might have noticed, let alone dared write; and if the simile isn't really confirmed by the footage – the tower's cladding would be its sheath, which didn't drop separately to reveal the building's body; further, as the building collapsed, smoke rose to conceal its downfall – it is, again, not a gaudy one-off, but an image with thematic resonance. That there can be beauty (and, for some, eroticism) in destruction is unarguable; and this moment links directly to the second episode of the story, a flashback to one of the hijackers drunkenly expounding his zealotry in a Florida strip club. After the imagined viewpoints of two victims (a man in the World Trade Center, a woman aboard the fourth plane pleading with the Lord for mercy), we rejoin Kellogg, six months later, to find he has now lost his atheism as he had previously lost his belief. Why? Because human consciousness always insists on narrative and meaning, and so, for him, on faith. The story is in part about levels of belief – like the levels of a skyscraper – from atheistic ground zero to a space close to the invisible godhead.

In one of his final poems, 'Peggy Lutz, Fred Muth', Updike

addresses both his old friends and fundamental source
material:

> *Dear friends of childhood, classmates, thank you,*
> *scant hundred of you, for providing a*
> *sufficiency of human types: beauty,*
> *bully, hanger-on, natural,*
> *twin, and fatso – all a writer needs,*
> *all there in Shillington, its trolley cars*
> *and little factories, cornfields and trees,*
> *leaf fires, snowflakes, pumpkins, valentines.*

Corroboration (if any were needed) comes in the title story
of the final collection, 'My Father's Tears', in which Jim (home
escaper/father of four/twice married/high-school reunionist)
is told by his second wife that his escape from his background
has only ever been partial: 'Sylvia . . . recognises that I have
never really left Pennsylvania, that it is where the self I valued
is stored, however infrequently I check on its condition.' Much
of this volume may be seen as a variegated checking on that
early, continuing soul. Jim's time and place – post-war Alton
– contained two iconic buildings: the old station where 'the
tall-backed waiting benches were as dignified as church pews',
and 'the stately Carnegie-endowed library two blocks down
Franklin Street'. Both, of course, are locations for escape. Also,
'both had been built for eternity, when railroads and books
looked to be with us forever'. Yet within a decade Alton's
station, 'like railroad stations all across the East, would be
padlocked and boarded up', awaiting its obliteration.

Implications about the Death of the Book, here merely
implied, are pessimistically clarified in 'The Author Observes
His Birthday, 2005':

> *A life poured into words – apparent waste*
> *intended to preserve the thing consumed.*

For who, in that unthinkable future
when I am dead, will read? The printed page
was just a half-millennium's brief wonder . . .

Perhaps; but there is way too much vitality in Updike (and in life, and literature, and the maligned book – and the reader) for that. 'My Father's Tears' cuts swiftly to the upcountry Vermont farmhouse belonging to Jim's first wife's family, where as a young husband he once observed a rare, ordinary phenomenon:

> The lone bathroom was a long room, its plaster walls and wooden floor both bare, that was haunted by a small but intense rainbow, which moved around the walls as the sun in the course of the day glinted at a changing angle off the bevelled edge of the mirror on the medicine cabinet. When we troubled to heat up enough water on the kerosene stove for a daylight bath, the prismatically generated rainbow kept the bather company; it quivered and bobbed when foot-steps or a breath of wind made the house tremble.

For Jim this 'Ariel-like phenomenon' has an extra resonance, since it was here, in the farmhouse, that his then wife first became pregnant: 'This microscopic event deep within my bride became allied in my mind with the little rainbow low on the bathroom wall, our pet imp of refraction.'

When Updike and John Cheever appeared together on *The Dick Cavett Show* in 1981 (their only joint TV appearance), the true fact of mutual admiration made for untypically quiet television: Updike at one point mused that Cavett must be regretting not having booked Mailer and Vidal instead. When Cavett pushed these two writers, whom ignorance sometimes lumped together, to describe their differences, Cheever said that Updike was the only writer he knew who gave a sense

of American lives being performed in an environment of a
grandeur that escaped them. In reply and counterpraise, Updike
emphasised that Cheever was a transcendentalist, feeling and
conveying a radiance which he, Updike, was unable to feel
and convey. Comparatively, this is the case; though in and by
himself Updike is, if not a transcendentalist, at least a trans-
formationist, looking for the rainbow in the bathroom, the
imp of refraction.

In his very last story, 'The Full Glass' (published in the
New Yorker on 26 May 2008), a former insurance salesman
turned floor sander, now approaching eighty, reviews his life
through the prism of water (the sea, the body's constitution,
human tears, the glass of the stuff he needs to swallow his
'life-prolonging pills'). Most people tend to see life as a glass
which is, according to temperament, half full or half empty.
This (for once unnamed) first-person narrator prefers to retrospect in terms of 'moments of that full-glass feeling'. The
story's last sentence, in which the narrator stands back and
looks at himself – or Updike stands back and looks at the
narrator, or Updike stands back and looks at himself – runs:
'If I can read this strange old guy's mind aright, he's drinking
a toast to the visible world, his impending disappearance from
it be damned.'

Impossible not to think of and feel for Updike as he
tapped out that sentence and then added his last full stop, his
fictional endpoint. Impossible equally not to honour and thank
him with a reader's raised glass, full to the brim – though
preferably not with water.

When a writer you admire dies, rereading seems a normal courtesy and tribute. Occasionally, it may be prudent to resist going back: when Lawrence Durrell died, I preferred to remain with forty-year-old memories of *The Alexandria Quartet* rather than risk such lushness again. And sometimes the nature of the writer's oeuvre creates a problem of choice. This was the case with John Updike. Should you choose one of his previously unopened books (in my case two dozen or so)? Or go for one you suspect you misread, or undervalued, at the time? Or one, like *Couples*, which you might have read at the time for somewhat non-literary reasons?

The decision eventually made itself. I had first read the Rabbit Quartet in the autumn of 1991, in what felt near-perfect circumstances. I was on a book tour of the States, and bought the first volume, *Rabbit, Run*, in a Penguin edition at Heathrow. I picked up the others in different American cities, in chunky Fawcett Crest paperbacks, and read them as I criss-crossed the country, my bookmarks the stubs of boarding passes. When released from publicity duties, I would either retreat inwards to Updike's prose, or outwards to walk ordinary American streets. This gave my reading, it felt, a deepening stereoscopy. And even when, too exhausted to do anything, I fell back on the hotel minibar and television, I found I was only replicating Harry 'Rabbit' Angstrom's preferred way of ingesting politics and current events. After three weeks, both Harry and I found ourselves in Florida, 'death's favourite state', as he puts it in the final volume, *Rabbit at Rest*. Harry died; the book ended; my tour was over.

I came home convinced that the Quartet was the best American novel of the post-war period. Nearly twenty years on, with Updike newly dead, and another American journey coming up, it was time to check on that judgement. By now those four volumes had, with a final authorial revision, been fused into a 1,516-page hardback under the overall title *Rabbit Angstrom*. If the protagonist's nickname denotes a zigzagging creature of impulse and appetite, the *angst* of his Scandinavian surname indicates that Harry is also the bearer of a more metaphysical burden. Not that he is more than fleetingly aware of it; and the fact that he isn't makes him all the more emblematically American.

Harry is a specific American, a high-school basketball star, department-store underling, linotype operator and finally Toyota car salesman in the decaying industrial town of Brewer, Pennsylvania (Updike based it on Reading, Pa., which he knew as a boy). Until Rabbit starts wintering in Florida in the final volume, he scarcely leaves Brewer – a location chosen to represent Middle America by a New York film company in *Rabbit Redux*. Harry is site-specific, slobbish, lust-driven, passive, patriotic, hard-hearted, prejudiced, puzzled, anxious. Yet familiarity renders him likeable – for his humour, his doggedness, his candour, his curiosity and his wrong-headed judgements (for example, preferring Perry Como to Sinatra). But Updike was disappointed when readers went further and claimed they found Rabbit lovable: 'My intention was never to make him – or any character – lovable.' Instead, Harry is typical, and it takes an outsider to tell him so. An Australian doctor asked by Janice what is wrong with Rabbit's dicky heart replies: 'The usual thing, ma'am. It's tired and stiff and full of crud. It's a typical American heart, for his age and economic status etcetera.' Harry's quiet role as an American everyman is publicly confirmed in *Rabbit at Rest* when he is chosen for his second, brief moment of public fame: dressing up as Uncle Sam for a town parade.

Rereading the Quartet, I was struck by how much of it is about running away: Harry, Janice and Nelson all take off at different points, and all return defeatedly. (Updike explained that *Rabbit, Run* was partly a riposte to Kerouac's *On the Road*, and intended as a 'realistic demonstration of what happens when a young American family man goes on the road' – i.e. the family gets hurt, and the deserter slinks home.) I had forgotten how harshly transactional much of the sex was; how increasingly droll Rabbit becomes as he ages (Reagan reminds him of God in that 'you never knew how much he knew, nothing or everything', while Judaism 'must be a great religion, once you get past the circumcision'); how masterfully Updike deploys free indirect style, switching us in and out of the main characters' consciousness; and how, instead of making each sequel merely sequential, he is constantly back-filling previous books with new information (the most extreme example being that we only get Janice's pre-Rabbit sexual history in the 2000 follow-up novella *Rabbit Remembered* – forty years after we might have learned it).

What I had never forgotten was the audacity of Updike's starting point. Harry is only twenty-six, but past it: his brief years of sporting fame lie behind him, and he is already bored with his wife Janice. On the second page, he refers to himself as 'getting old' – and there are still several hundred thousand words to go. Even when he attains bovine contentment and material success in *Rabbit is Rich*, it is against a general background of things being over before they have really begun. Each book is purposefully set at the dying of a decade – from the fifties to the eighties – so there is little wider sense of fresh beginnings: the Sixties America of *Rabbit Redux* isn't filled with love and peace and hopefulness, but with hatred, violence and craziness as the decade sours and dies. Perhaps America is itself dying, or at least being outpaced by the world: this is what Harry, and the novel, both wonder. What is American power if it can be defeated by the Vietcong; what is American inventiveness if it can be out-invented by the Japanese; what is American wealth when national debt piles up? In *Rabbit Redux* Harry feels he has 'come in on the end' of the American dream, 'as the world shrank like an apple going bad'; by the start of *Rabbit is Rich* he feels 'the great American ride is ending'; by the end of *Rabbit at Rest* 'the whole free world is wearing out'.

Whereas in my first reading I was overwhelmed by Updike's joy of description, his passionate attentiveness to such things as 'the clunky suck of the refrigerator door opening and shutting' – by what he called, in the preface to his *Early Stories*, 'giving the mundane its beautiful due' – in my second I was increasingly aware of this underlying sense of things being already over, of the tug of dying and death. Thus the whole trajectory of Janice's life is an attempt to expiate the sin of having accidentally, drunkenly, drowned her baby. And while Harry imagines himself a genial and harmless life-enhancer, others see him quite differently. 'Boy, you really have the touch of death, don't you?' his sort-of-whore girlfriend Ruth says at the end of *Rabbit, Run*. 'Hold still. Just sit there. I see you very clear all of a sudden. You're Mr Death himself.' Harry's son Nelson agrees with this analysis. In *Rabbit Redux*, Harry is away on another sexual escapade when his house burns down, killing the runaway hippie Jill; teenage Nelson, equally smitten by the girl, thereafter treats his father as a simple murderer. And in *Rabbit at Rest* Harry fears his female-killing curse is striking a third time when his rented Sunfish capsizes and his granddaughter Judy is nowhere to be seen. This time, as it happens, the hex is reversed: Judy is only hiding beneath the sail, and the scare triggers Rabbit's first heart attack, a dry run for his death.

And after death? Harry's intimations, not of immortality, but of the numinous, show up more clearly on rereading. Updike said that he couldn't quite give up on religion, because without the possibility or dream of something beyond and above, our terrestrial life became unendurable. Rabbit shares this vestigial need. 'I don't *not* believe,' he assures his dying lover Thelma, who replies, 'That's not quite enough, I fear. Harry, darling.' But it's all he can manage: 'Hell, what I think about religion is . . . is without a little of it, you'll sink.' But this 'little' doesn't find or express itself, as did Updike's, in churchgoing. God-believers in the Quartet tend to be either crazies like Skeeter, fanatics, or pious post-Narcotics Anonymous droners like Nelson. Harry is not exactly a joined-up thinker, but he has an occasionally questing mind, a sense of what it might be if there were something beyond our heavy-footed sublunary existence. It's perhaps significant that the sport at which he excelled, which he plays in both the opening and closing pages of the tetralogy, involves a leaving of the ground and a reaching-up to something higher, if only to a skirted hoop. A greater reaching-up is offered by the US space programme, whose achievements (and failures, as in the *Challenger* mission) run through the book; Harry has a couch potato's fascination for it – as he does for the fate of the Dalai Lama, with whom he bizarrely, mock-heroically identifies. But there are also moments when he is able to recognise his longings more precisely. Beside the big stucco house belonging to Janice's parents there grew a large copper beech, which for many years shaded Harry and Janice's bedroom. When Nelson comes into occupation of the family house, in *Rabbit at Rest*, he has the tree cut down. Harry doesn't argue; nor can he 'tell the boy that the sound of the rain in that great beech had been the most religious experience of his life. That, and hitting a pure golf shot.' In such moments Rabbit exemplifies a kind of suburban pantheism, giving the mundane its spiritual due.

Rabbit Angstrom has its imperfections. The second volume is usually considered the weakest of the four; and it's true that Skeeter's mau-mauing of whitey Rabbit goes on too long, and to decreasing effect; a weakness perhaps ascribable to

Updike's authorial glee at having found the voice, and then getting carried away by it. And there is a change in register after the first volume, where the hushed Joyceanism of his early mode – when he thought of himself as a short-story writer and poet, but not yet fully as a novelist – is to the fore. (Updike didn't realise that he was heading towards a tetralogy until after the second volume.) On the other hand, it's rare for a work of this length to get even better as it goes on, with *Rabbit at Rest* the strongest and richest of the four books. In the last hundred pages or so, I found myself slowing deliberately, not so much because I didn't want the book to end, as because I didn't want Rabbit to die. (And when he does, his last words, to his shrieking son, are, maybe, also addressed consolingly to the reader: 'All I can tell you is, it isn't so bad.') Any future historian wanting to understand the texture, smell, feel and meaning of bluey-white-collar life in ordinary America between the 1950s and the 1990s will need little more than the Rabbit Quartet. But that implies only sociological rather than artistic virtue. So let's just repeat: still the greatest post-war American novel.

REGULATING SORROW

I N HIS ESSAY 'The Proper Means of Regulating Sorrow'
(*The Rambler*, 28 August 1750), Dr Johnson identifies the
dreadful uniqueness of grief among the human passions.
Ordinary desires, virtuous or vicious, contain within them the
theoretical possibility of their satisfaction:

> The miser always imagines that there is a certain sum
> that will fill his heart to the brim; and every ambitious
> man, like King Pyrrhus, has an acquisition in his
> thoughts that is to terminate his labours, after which
> he shall pass the rest of his life in ease or gaity, in
> repose or devotion.

But grief, or 'sorrow', is different in kind. Even with painful
passions – fear, jealousy, anger – nature always suggests to us
a solution, and with it an end to that oppressive feeling:

> But for sorrow there is no remedy provided by nature.
> It is often occasioned by accidents irreparable, and
> dwells upon objects that have lost or changed their
> existence. It requires what it cannot hope, that the
> laws of the universe should be repealed, that the dead
> should return, or the past should be recalled.

Unless we have a religious belief which envisages the total
resurrection of the body, we know that we shall never see the
lost loved again on terrestrial terms: never see, never talk and

listen to, never touch, never hold. In the quarter of a millennium since Johnson described the unparalleled pain of grief, we – we in the secularising West, at least – have got less good at dealing with death, and therefore with its emotional consequences. Of course, at one level we know that we all shall die; but death has come to be looked upon more as a medical failure than a human norm. It increasingly happens away from the home, in hospital, and is handled by a series of outside specialists – a matter for the professionals. But afterwards we, the amateurs, the grief-struck, are left to deal with it – this unique, banal thing – as best we can. And there are now fewer social forms to surround and support the grief-bearer. Very little is handed down from one generation to the next about what it is like. We are expected to suffer in comparative silence; being 'strong' is the template; wailing and weeping a sign of 'giving in to grief', which is held by some to be a bad way of 'dealing with it'. Of course, there is the love of family and friends to fall back on, but they may know less than we do, and their concerned phrases – 'It *does* get better'; 'Two years is what they say'; 'You *are* looking more yourself' – are often based on uncertain authority and general hopefulness. Foreign travel is advised; so is getting a dog. Other, supposedly parallel cases of loss and grief are helpfully cited; occasionally they seem insulting, but mostly just irrelevant. As Forster wrote in *Howards End*: 'One death may explain itself, but it throws no light upon another.'

Death sorts people out: both the grief-bearers, and those around them. As the survivor's life is forcibly recalibrated, friendships are often tested; some pass, some fail. Men are generally more awkward, more silent, more useless than women. Odd phenomena occur: co-grievers may indulge in the phenomenon of competitive mourning – I loved him/her more, and with these extra tears of mine I'll prove it. As for the sorrowing relics – widow, widower or unwed partner – they can become morbidly sensitive, easily moved to anger by too much intrusiveness or too much distance-keeping; by too many words or too few. They may also experience a strange competitiveness of their own: an irrational need to prove (to whom?) that their grief is the larger, the heavier, the purer (than whose?).

A friend of mine, widowed in his sixties, told me, 'This is a crappy age for it to happen.' Meaning, I think, that if the catastrophe had happened in his seventies, he could have settled in and waited for death; whereas if it had happened in his fifties, he might have been able to restart his life. But every age is a crappy age for it to happen, and there is no correct answer in that game of would-you-rather? How do you compare the grief of a young parent left with small children to that of an aged person amputated from his or her partner of fifty or sixty years? There is no hierarchy to grief, except in the matter of feeling. Another friend of mine, widowed in a moment after fifty years of marriage – the knot of travellers by a baggage carousel in the arrivals hall turned out to be surrounding her suddenly-dead husband – wrote to me: 'Nature is very exact in the matter. It hurts just as much as it is worth.'

Joan Didion had been married to John Gregory Dunne for forty years when he died in mid-sentence while on his second pre-dinner whisky in December 2003. Joyce Carol Oates and Raymond Smith had been together for 'forty-seven years and twenty-five days' when Smith, in hospital but apparently recovering well from pneumonia, was swept away by a secondary infection in February 2008. Both literary couples were intensely close yet non-competitive, often working in the same space and rarely apart: in the case of Didion–Dunne, for a 'week or two or three here and there when one of us was doing a piece'; in the case of Oates–Smith, for never more than a day or two. Didion realised after Dunne's death that 'I had no letters from John, not one' (she does not say if he had any from her); while Oates and Smith 'had no correspondence. Not once had we written to each other.' The similarities continue: in each marriage the woman was the star; each of the dead husbands had been a lapsed Catholic; neither wife seems to have imagined in advance her transformation into widow; and each left her husband's voice on the answering machine for some while after his death. Further, each survivor decided to chronicle her first year of widowhood, and each of their books was completed within those twelve months.

Yet Oates's *A Widow's Story* and Didion's *The Year of Magical Thinking* couldn't be more different. Though Didion's opening lines (the fourth of which is 'The question of self-pity') were jotted down a day or two after Dunne's death, she waited eight months before beginning to write. Oates's book is largely based on diary entries, most from the earliest part of her year: so in a 415-page book, we find that by page 125 we have covered just a week of her widowhood, and by page 325 are still only at week eight. While both books are autobiographies, Didion is essayistic and concise, seeking external points of comparison, trying to set her case in some wider context. Oates is novelistic and expansive, switching between first and third persons, seeking (not with unfailing success) to objectify herself as 'the widow'; and though she occasionally reaches for the handholds of Pascal, Nietzsche, Emily Dickinson, Crashaw and William Carlos Williams, she is mainly focused on the dark interiors, the psycho-chaos of grief. Each writer, in other words, is playing to her strengths.

That both Didion and Oates limit their books to the first year of their widowhoods is logical. Long-married couples develop a certain rhythm, gravity and coloration to the annual cycle, and so those first twelve months propose at every turn a terrible choice: between doing the same as last year, only this time by yourself, or deliberately not doing the same as last year, and thereby perhaps feeling even more by yourself. That first year contains many stations of the cross. Learning to return to a silent, empty house. Learning to avoid what Oates calls 'sinkholes' – those 'places fraught with visceral memory'. Learning how to balance necessary solitude and necessary gregariousness. Learning how to react to friends who are mystifyingly unable to mention the name of the lost partner; or colleagues who fail to find the right words, like the 'Princeton acquaintance' who greeted Oates 'with an air of hearty reproach', and the line, 'Writing up a storm, eh, Joyce?' Or like the woman friend who offers her the consolation that grief 'is neurological. Eventually the neurons are "recircuited". I would think that, if this is so, you could speed up the process by just *knowing*.' The intention is kindly; the effect, patronising. Oh, so it's just a question of waiting for one's neurons to settle? Then there are practical problems: for instance, the garden your husband lovingly tended, but in which you are less interested; you may enjoy the results, but rarely joined him in visits to the garden centre. So do you faithfully replicate the same work, or do you unfaithfully let the garden look after itself? Here, Oates finds a wise third way: where Smith planted only annuals, she replants with nothing but perennials, asking the nurseryman for 'Anything that requires a minimum of work and is guaranteed to survive'.

Which is the problem confronting the widow: how to survive that first year, how to turn into a perennial. This involves surmounting fears and anxieties for which there is no training. Previously, Oates rated as 'the most exquisite of intimacies' the ability to occupy the same space as Ray for hours, without the need to speak; now, there is a quite different order of silence. 'What I am', Oates writes, 'begins to be revealed now that I am alone. In such revelation is terror.' At one point she thinks 'half-seriously of sending an email to friends' asking if she might hire one of them 'if you could overcome the scruples of friendship and allow me to pay you in some actual way – to keep me alive for a year, at least?' She wants to be a 'good widow' and asserts that 'I will do what Ray would want me to do', while also – classically – blaming Ray for having put her in this state; she is sleepless and irritable; she envisages her grief and insomnia lasting for a decade, while also doubting that her mourning is 'real'. She muses on suicide, though more in a theoretical than practical way – while also knowing that 'thinking seriously of suicide is a deterrent to suicide'. She finds that work comes much harder, noting of a new short story that it 'will require literally weeks' (a complaint that will make most other writers chuckle). And, like many of the grief-struck, she fears for her own mental state: 'Half the time, I think I must be totally out of my mind.' Oates excellently conveys the disconnect between the inwardly chaotic self and the outwardly functioning person (and she *is* functioning again with remarkable rapidity – correcting proofs and working on a story within a week of Smith's death, back on the promotional road within three). She is certainly less in control than she seems to outsiders, but probably more in control than she feels to herself. The grief-struck frequently act in ways that could be seen as either half sane or half mad, but rarely give themselves the benefit of the doubt. For instance, the day after Ray's death, Oates goes to their bedroom closet and throws out not her husband's clothes, but half of *her own* clothes. She does it as punishment for her vanity, and because these garments speak of a time when she wore them happily with Ray – so now they have no meaning or merit. It is in such moments of rational irrationality that the nature of grief is made plain to us.

Most of the grief-struck suffer – especially in the first months – from a terror of forgetting their lost one. Often the shock of death wipes out the memory of earlier times, and there is a morbid fear that it will never be recovered: that the lost one will now be twice lost, twice killed. Joyce Carol Oates does not appear to have suffered this fear; instead, she suffers a rarer, more interesting and potentially more corrosive one

– that of never having fully known her husband in the first place. Oates and Smith married in January 1961, and her portrait of their first years together – the time when secrets are exchanged, concentration on the other is at its fullest, and the lineaments and rules of the partnership are worked out – is both vivid and touching. It is also a relationship coloured more by the 1950s than the 1960s. Oates was eight years younger than Smith; they were shy of one another, even in marriage; by her own account she never wanted to upset him, let alone argue with him. Thus, for example:

> It was years before I summoned up the courage to suggest to Ray that I did not really like some of the music he frequently played on our stereo – such macho-hectic compositions as Prokofiev's *Alexander Nevsky*, the chorale ending of Beethoven's *Ninth Symphony* with its relentless *joy joy joy* like spikes hammered into the skull, much of Mahler . . .

Fortunately, it seems that Smith was only in touch with the 'macho-hectic' side of masculinity when lowering a stylus onto vinyl. He comes across as quiet, loyal and domesticated; a cook, a keen gardener and a meticulous editor of the *Ontario Review*. He read most of his wife's non-fiction but very little of her fiction. It is, of course, a famously large oeuvre (fifty-five novels plus hundreds of short stories); even so, the reader is brought up short when Oates writes: 'I don't believe that Ray read my first novel *With Shuddering Fall*.' Which is the more astonishing: that he didn't read it, that she isn't sure whether or not he did, or that she expresses neither annoyance nor disappointment at his omission? But then her opinions on the relationship between the sexes are somewhat unusual:

> To a woman, the quintessential male is unknowable, elusive.

In our marriage, it was our practice not to share anything that was upsetting, depressing, demoralizing, tedious – unless it was unavoidable.

Women are inclined to console men, all women, all men, in all circumstances without discretion.

The ideal marriage is of a writer and his/her editor.

A wife must respect her husband's family even when – as sometimes happens – her husband does not entirely respect them.

A wife must respect the *otherness* of her husband – she must accept it, she will never know him fully.

This sounds like shyness raised to marital principle; and it brings with it the danger that when the wife becomes a widow and goes through her husband's papers, she will find out things she barely suspected. In Ray Smith's case: a nervous breakdown, a love affair at a sanitarium, a psychiatrist's description of him as 'love-starved', and further evidence of a difficult, distant relationship with his father. 'For all that I knew Ray so well,' she concludes, 'I didn't know his *imagination*.' Nor, perhaps, did he know hers, given that he rarely read her fiction. But he was 'the first man in my life, the last man, the only man'.

In some ways, autobiographical accounts of grief are unfalsifiable, and therefore unreviewable by any normal criteria. The book is repetitive? So is grief. The book is obsessive? So is grief. The book is at times incoherent? So is grief. Phrases like 'Friends have been wonderful inviting me to their homes' are platitudes; but grief is filled with platitudes. The chapter headed 'Fury!' opens:

Then suddenly, I am so angry.
I am so very very angry, I am furious.
I am sick with fury, like a wounded animal.
A kick of adrenaline to the heart, my heart begins thudding rapid and furious as a fist slamming against an obdurate surface – a locked door, a wall.

If a creative writing student turned this in as part of a story, the professor might reach for her red pencil; but if that same professor is writing a stream-of-consciousness diary about grief, the paragraph becomes strangely validated. This *is* how it feels, and what is grief at times but a car-crash of cliché? A few pages later, Oates is reflecting on the fact that she now has a private identity as 'Joyce Smith' or 'Mrs Smith', official widow, and a public identity under her full three-part writing name:

> 'Oates' is an island, an oasis, to which on this agitated morning I can row, as in an uncertain little skiff, with an unwieldy paddle – the way is arduous not because the water is deep but because the water is shallow and weedy and the bottom of the skiff is endangered by the rocks beneath. And yet – once I have rowed to this island, this oasis, this core of calm amid the chaos of my life – once I arrive at the University . . .

The image of a skiff and a water-crossing is dead and unrevivable, no matter how extended? It doesn't matter. This sentence may be the first in world literature where the writer imagines you can row to an oasis? But you don't understand: incoherence of imagery is a fair representation of the acutely distracted and fractured mind. You mean, she didn't even notice when reading the proofs? Again, it doesn't matter whether she did or didn't. You asked for a sense of what it is like: *this* is what it is like.

Grief dislocates both space and time. The grief-struck find themselves in a new geography, where other people's maps are only ever approximate. Time also ceases to be reliable. C. S. Lewis, in *A Grief Observed*, describes the effect on him of his wife's death:

> Up till this I always had too little time. Now there is nothing but time. Almost pure time. Empty successiveness.

And this unreliability of time adds to the confusion in the sorrower's mind as to whether grief is a state or a process. This is far from a theoretical matter. It is at the heart of the question: Will it always be like this? Will things get better? Why should they? And if so, how will I be able to tell? Lewis admits that when he started writing his book,

> I thought I could describe a *state*; make a map of sorrow. Sorrow, however, turns out to be not a state but a process. It needs not a map but a history.

Probably, it needs both at the same time. We might try to pin it down by saying that grief is the state and mourning the process; yet to the person enduring one or both, things are rarely so clear, and the 'process' is one which involves much slipping-back into the paralysis of the 'state'. There are various objective markers: the point at which tears – regular, daily tears – stop; the point when the brain returns to quasi-normal functioning; the point when possessions are disposed of; the point when memory of the lost one begins to return. But there can be no general rules, nor standard timescale. Those pesky neurons just can't be relied upon.

What happens next, when the state and the process are, if by no means complete, at least established and recognisable? What happens to our heart? Again, there are those confident surrounding voices (from 'How could he/she ever marry again after living with her/him?' to 'They say the happily married tend to remarry quickly, often within six months'). A friend whose long-term lover had died of Aids told me, 'There's only one upside to this thing: you can do what you fucking well like.' The trouble is, that when you are in sorrow, most notions of 'what you like' will contain the presence of your lost love and the impossible demand that the laws of the universe be repealed. And so: a hunkering-down, a closing-off, a retreat into the posthumous faithfulness of memory? Raymond Smith didn't much like Dr Johnson, finding him too didactic, and preferring the Doctor of Boswell's account to that of his own writings. But on sorrow, Johnson is not so much didactic as wise, clear and decisive:

> An attempt to preserve life in a state of neutrality and indifference is unreasonable and vain. If by excluding joy we could shut out grief, the scheme would deserve very serious attention. But since, however we may debar ourselves from happiness, misery will find its way at many inlets, and the assaults of pain will force our regard, though we may withhold it from the invitations of pleasure, we may surely endeavour to raise life above the middle point of apathy at one time, since it will be necessary to sink below it at another.

So what constitutes 'success' in mourning? The ability to return to concentration and work; the ability to rediscover interest in life, and take pleasure in it, while recognising that present pleasure is far from past joy. The ability to hold the lost love successfully in mind, remembering without distorting. The ability to continue living as he or she would have wanted you to do (though this is a tricky area, where the sorrowful can often end up giving themselves a free pass). And then what? Some form of self-sufficiency which avoids neutrality and indifference? Or a new relationship that will either supplant the lost one or, perhaps, draw strength from it?

There is another strange parallel between *The Year of Magical Thinking* and *A Widow's Story*. By the time each book came out, many readers would know one additional key fact not covered by the text. In Didion's case, the death of her daughter Quintana (which the author deals with in a subsequent edition); in Oates's, her remarriage to a neuroscientist, whose existence is hinted at rather coyly on the last page. You could argue that those writing about grief make their own literary terms more than most; but even so, in Oates's case there is something unhappy in the omission. She is writing about the twelve months that began on 18 February 2008; we know from her own mouth (in an interview with *The Times*) that she met her second husband in August 2008, they started going on walks and hikes in September, and were married in March 2009. If Didion posed 'the question of self-pity' in the first lines of her book, Oates, in a chapter called 'Taboo', similarly approaches the difficult heart of the matter:

> It's a taboo subject. How *the dead* are betrayed by the living. We who are living − we who have survived − understand that our guilt is what links us to the dead. At all times we can hear them calling to us, a growing incredulity in their voices. *You will not forget me − will you? How can you forget me? I have no one but you.*

But the theme is no sooner announced than set aside; indeed, when Oates comes back to the idea of 'betraying' her husband, it is in the much narrower context of disclosing to the reader secrets about Ray Smith's family and upbringing. But she does this, she explains, because 'There is no purpose to a memoir, if it isn't honest. As there is no purpose to a declaration of love, if it isn't honest.' Her book ends with a chapter headed 'The Widow's Handbook' which reads in its entirety:

> Of the widow's countless death-duties there is really just one that matters: on the anniversary of her husband's death the widow should think *I kept myself alive*.

But if she is also thinking 'I might be getting married in a few weeks' time', does this not change the nature of that statement? This isn't a moral comment: Oates may quote Marianne Moore's line that 'the cure for loneliness is solitude', but many people need to be married, and therefore, at times, remarried. However, some readers will feel they have a good case for breach of narrative promise. Was not Ray 'the first man in my life, the last man, the only man'? And what about all those perennials she planted?

When Dr Johnson wrote 'The Proper Means of Regulating Sorrow' he was not yet widowed. That event was to occur two years later, when he was forty-three. Twenty-eight years afterwards, in a letter of consolation to Dr Thomas Lawrence, whose wife had recently died, Johnson wrote:

> He that outlives a wife whom he has long loved, sees himself disjoined from the only mind that has the same hopes, and fears, and interest; from the only companion with whom he has shared much good or evil; and with whom he could set his mind at liberty, to retrace the past, or anticipate the future. The continuity of being is lacerated; the settled course of sentiment and action is stopped; and life stands suspended and motionless, till it is driven by external causes into a new channel. But the time of suspense is dreadful.

ACKNOWLEDGEMENTS

Original versions of these pieces appeared as follows:

Fitzgerald: *Guardian*, 26 July 2008.
Clough: Persephone Books, 2009.
Orwell: *New York Review of Books*, 12 March 2009.
Ford and *The Good Soldier*: *New York Review of Books*, 9 January 1997.
Ford in Provence: *Guardian*, 21 August 2010.
Parade's End: Penguin Books, 2012.
Kipling's France: *Guardian*, 11 November 2003.
France's Kipling: *Guardian*, 5 November 2005.
Chamfort: *Guardian*, 4 October 2003.
Mérimée: *Guardian*, 7 July 2007.
Fénéon: *London Review of Books*, 4 October 2007.
Houellebecq: *New Yorker*, 7 July 2003.
Translating *Madame Bovary*: *London Review of Books*, 18 November 2010.
Wharton: Everyman's Library, 1996.
Hemingway: *New Yorker*, 4 July 2011.
Moore: *New York Review of Books*, 22 October 1998.
Updike: *New York Review of Books*, 11 June 2009; *Guardian*, 17 October 2009.
Oates: *New York Review of Books*, 7 April 2011.

INDEX